CAMBRIDGE

CW00821257

First for Schools

TRAINER

SIX PRACTICE TESTS WITHOUT ANSWERS

2

Cambridge University Press
www.cambridge.org/elt

Cambridge Assessment English
www.cambridgeenglish.org

Information on this title: www.cambridge.org/9781009212175

© Cambridge University Press & Assessment and UCLES 2018

First published 2018
This edition published in 2022

20 19 18 17 16 15 14 13 12 11 10 9 8 7 6 5 4

Printed in the Netherlands by Wilco BV

A catalogue record for this publication is available from the British Library

ISBN 978-1-009-21217-5 Six Practice Tests without Answers with eBook
ISBN 978-1-009-21216-8 Six Practice Tests with Answers and Teacher's Notes with eBook

Contents

Introduction

Who is this book for?

If you are aged between 12 and 16 and want to take *Cambridge English: First for Schools (FCE)*, this book is for you!

Why is this book called 'Trainer'?

This book is called '**Trainer**' because it is full of exercises to help you get better and better at doing each part of *Cambridge English: First for Schools*.
So, complete all the exercises then do all the practice papers! If you train and work hard, you'll soon be ready to take *Cambridge English: First for Schools*.

How do I use this book?

First, do the grammar and vocabulary exercises on each **Training** page. Then do the task on the **Exam practice** page and check your answers.

On Training pages you will find:

 Cambridge Learner Corpus

This shows information about mistakes that some *Cambridge English: First for Schools* candidates make. If you do these useful exercises, you will learn <u>not</u> to make these mistakes when <u>you</u> do *Cambridge English: First for Schools*.

The authors used the Corpus to see how English is really used and to identify typical learner mistakes.

 Tip!

These are ideas to help you do well in the exam. For example: *You may find that Listening Part 3 options include adjectives to describe the speaker's feelings, which you then have to match carefully to what the speaker says.*

Remember!

These are quick hints about grammar points or vocabulary that you should learn.
For example:
To change **direct questions** to **indirect questions**:
Wh- questions: **What's** the time? → Do you know **what** the time **is**?
Yes/No questions: **Is** John here? → Do you know **if** John **is** here?

On Exam practice pages you will find:

- a *Cambridge English: First for Schools* **exam task** for you to try and complete
- **advice** to help you with different parts of the task.

Tests 3, 4, 5 and 6:

When you finish Tests 1 and 2 you will be ready to do complete *Cambridge English: First for Schools* **practice tests**.

Tests 3, 4, 5 and 6 are just like real *Cambridge English: First for Schools* Reading and Use of English, Writing, Listening and Speaking papers. Doing these tests will give you extra help to prepare for the exam.

Keep a record of your scores as you do the tests. You may find that your scores are good in some parts of the test but you may need to practise other parts more. Make simple tables like this to help record your scores.

Paper 3 Listening

	Part 1	Part 2	Part 3	Part 4
Test 3				
Test 4				
Test 5				
Test 6				

Other features of the First for Schools Trainer

- **Visual material**

In the Speaking test the examiner will give you a booklet with pictures and photographs in it. The visual material in the colour section from pages C1–C24 will help you practise and become familiar with the type of photographs and written questions you will see in the test and help you increase your confidence.

- **Answer sheets**

Look at these to see what the *Cambridge English: First for Schools* answer sheets in the test look like and learn how to complete them. Ask your teacher to photocopy them so that you can use them when you do your practice tests.

- **Downloadable audio online**

Listen to these to practise the Listening paper. You will need to listen to these to practise some parts of the Speaking paper too.

Cambridge English: First for Schools

Contents

Cambridge English: First for Schools has four papers:

Reading and Use of English: 1 hour 15 minutes

The paper contains seven parts. For Parts 1 to 3, the test contains texts with grammar and vocabulary tasks. Part 4 has separate items with a grammar and vocabulary focus. For Parts 5 to 7, the test contains a range of texts and reading comprehension tasks

Writing: 1 hour 20 minutes

The paper contains two parts. You will have to complete two tasks: a compulsory one in Part 1 and one from a choice of four in Part 2. Each question on this paper carries equal marks.

Listening: about 40 minutes

The paper contains four parts. The text types are *monologues* (answerphone messages, information lines, commentaries, radio documentaries and features, instructions, lectures, news, public announcements, advertisements, reports, speeches, stories and anecdotes, talks) and *interacting speakers* (conversations, discussions, interviews, quizzes, radio plays, transactions). For each correct answer you will receive one mark.

Speaking: 14 minutes

The Speaking test contains four parts: short conversations with one examiner and another student; a one-minute 'long turn' on your own; a task where you speak with the other student; and a discussion. Usually you will take the Speaking test with just one other student, but sometimes students take the Speaking test in groups of three (only when there's an odd number at the end of the session – it isn't an option normally). You will be marked on your performance throughout the test.

Frequently asked questions:

What level is *Cambridge English: First for Schools?*

At this level you should be able to:

● use the main structures of the language with some confidence
● demonstrate knowledge of a wide range of vocabulary
● use appropriate strategies to communicate in a variety of social situations
● pick out facts from spoken language and written text
● understand the difference between main points and other points
● understand the difference between the main idea of a text and specific detail
● produce written texts of various types showing that you can develop an argument as well as describe or retell events.

What grade do I need to pass *Cambridge English: First for Schools?*

Results are reported as three passing grades (A, B and C) and two failing grades (D and E). If you don't get a passing grade but show that you have ability in English at a slightly lower level (Council of Europe Level B1) you will get level B1 on your certificate. If you score below level B1 you will get a fail grade.

Basic user		Independent user		Proficient user	
A1	**A2**	**B1**	**B2**	**C1**	**C2**
	Key for Schools (KET for Schools)	Preliminary for Schools (PET for Schools)	First for Schools (FCE for Schools)		

What marks *do* I need to pass each paper, and to get an A or B in the exam?

You do not have to get a certain mark to pass each paper in the test. The final mark for *Cambridge English: First for Schools* is the total number of marks from all four papers: Reading and Use of English, Writing, Listening, and Speaking. The Reading and Use of English paper carries 40% of the marks, while Writing, Listening, and Speaking each carry 20% of the marks. You will receive a graph showing the results and a score for each paper out of 100. This means that the mark you need to pass the test will always be 60.

Grade A = 80–100   Grade B = 75–79   Grade C = 60–74

How can I find out about how I did in *each* paper of *Cambridge English: First for Schools?*

Before you get a certificate you will get the Statement of Results telling you how well you did in *Cambridge English: First for Schools*. As well as your result and your score out of 100 it also gives you your 'Candidate Profile'. This is an easy-to-read graph that shows how well you did on all the papers of the test compared to the all the other students taking the same test. If you do not get the score that you wanted, the Candidate Profile will show you which of the skills (reading and use of English, writing, listening or speaking) you did well in and which you need to improve.

Is *Cambridge English: First for Schools* appropriate for students of any age?

Cambridge English: First for Schools is more appropriate for students who are at school and aged from 12–16 but it is generally suited to students who are still at school who want to start working in an English-speaking environment or study at an upper-intermediate level. To make sure that the material is interesting for your age group and not too difficult or too easy for the B2 level, all the parts of the papers are pre-tested. This means that different groups of students try the materials for each part of the test first. The material will then only be used in real exams if the results of the pre-test show that it is appropriate for students who want to take *Cambridge English: First for Schools*.

> Can I use pens and pencils in the exam?

In *Cambridge English: First for Schools* students must use **pencil** in all the papers. It's useful for you if you want to change one of your answers on the answer sheet.

> What happens if I don't have enough time to finish writing?

You can only be given marks for what you write on your answer sheet, so if you do not complete this then you will miss the chance to show the examiner what you can do and how good your English is. Watch the clock and plan your time carefully. Do not waste time writing your answers on other pieces of paper. However, in the Listening test it is a good idea to write your answers on the question paper first. You will have time at the end to move your answers from the question paper to your answer sheet.

> If I write in capital letters, will it affect my score?

No. You do not lose marks for writing in capital letters in *Cambridge English: First for Schools*. Whether you choose to use capital letters or not, you should always make sure that your handwriting is clear and easy to read. Remember that the examiners can't mark a piece of writing that they can't read!

Note that different students have different strengths and weaknesses. Some may be good at speaking but not so good at writing; others may be good at reading but not so good at listening. The B2 Level 'Can Do' statements simply help teachers understand what *Cambridge English: First for Schools* candidates should generally be able to do at this level.

For more information on 'Can Do' statements go to:
http://www.cambridgeesol.org/images/28906-alte-can-do-document.pdf

In this part you:

- **read**   a text with eight gaps
- **choose**   from four options (**A, B, C** or **D**) to fill each gap

Useful language   Prepositional phrases

1   Which prepositions – *in*, *on*, *at* or *under* – can be used to complete the underlined phrases?

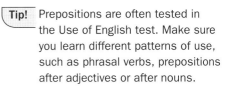

Tip! Prepositions are often tested in the Use of English test. Make sure you learn different patterns of use, such as phrasal verbs, prepositions after adjectives or after nouns.

   1 .... <u>the current rules</u> you are not allowed to wear shorts to school, although that will change from next year.

   2 Are you sure the deadline is next week? I was .... <u>the impression</u> it was today.

   3 We need to be .... <u>the road</u> by 7 a.m. or we'll never get to the train station on time.

   4 The football stadium is .... <u>the north</u> of the city, near the train station.

   5 Exam candidates must remain in their seats .... <u>all times</u>.

   6 The number of lions in the wild has been .... <u>decline</u> for many years.

   7 .... <u>the end of the day</u>, it makes no difference whether you pass your driving test or not because you can't afford to buy a car!

   8 Maria is .... <u>pressure</u> because her grades for last term were poor.

   9 Noel couldn't believe it when he arrived at school and saw the science lab was .... <u>fire</u>.

   10 .... <u>first</u>, Luisa thought everyone had forgotten about her birthday, but then she saw the big cake on the table.

2   Complete the text with *in*, *on*, *at* or *under*.

What to do if ...

Welcome to the blog where I give you advice on how to approach changes and issues **(1)** .... your everyday life. The topic of this week's blog is: **What to do if you move to a new school**.

There are many things you should do **(2)** .... the first day, and **(3)** .... the first week and during the first term. But there are things to do even before you start your new school.

First, you should visit the school. Go with your parents and have a look around. Find out where your classroom is going to be, where the canteen is and how to get to the toilets. If you know all this, you won't find yourself **(4)** .... a difficult situation where you need to ask for help.

When you are visiting your new school, try to speak to your teachers **(5)** .... the same time. It will help you get to know them, but perhaps more importantly, it will help them to find out a bit about you.

Nowadays, most schools have a handbook **(6)** .... the internet. Make sure you read it to find out about uniforms, what to do if you are sick or when exams are scheduled.

Follow these tips and it will help you feel that everything is **(7)** .... control when you start your first day. Find more help and advice for your first term by clicking on the links below.

Useful language Verb collocations

3 Choose the correct verb in *italics* that goes with each <u>underlined</u> phrase.

1 I usually *go / come* <u>for a swim</u> early in the morning before school.

2 If you forget to bring your project to school tomorrow, your history teacher will *go / get* <u>annoyed</u>.

3 The house *got / caught* <u>fire</u> early in the morning.

4 I love the colours of your clothes! Those colours really *go / get* <u>well together</u>.

5 The burglar was *caught / got* <u>in the act</u>. The police saw him coming out of the house with the TV at 4 a.m.

6 I *gave / got* my geography teacher <u>a good answer</u>, but it wasn't the answer he was looking for.

7 After a long discussion, Martha and her parents *got / came* <u>to a compromise</u> about what time she would come home after the party.

8 We're *getting / being* <u>together</u> after school to work on the history project. Do you want to join us?

9 My dream of playing in a band *went / came* <u>to life</u> when I started to write songs with some school friends.

10 Hannah is *giving / catching* <u>a party</u> to celebrate her 15th birthday next week.

4 Complete the sentences with the verb (A, B, C or D) which best fits each gap.

1 The school is trying to .... participation in extra-curricular activities like the chess team.

   A gain   **B** increase   **C** put up   **D** access

2 Would anyone else like to .... their opinion?

   A make   **B** take   **C** tell   **D** give

3 Did you manage to .... sight of the new sports car at the motor exhibition over the weekend?

   A catch   **B** find   **C** see   **D** discover

4 Jo was very upset to .... last in the 400 metres race despite all the hard training.

   A come   **B** end   **C** go   **D** become

5 Alexis .... his plans to leave the club at a team meeting.

   A called   **B** proposed   **C** announced   **D** told

6 After .... her bus for the third time that week, Elena knew she was going to be in trouble.

   A missing   **B** losing   **C** failing   **D** forgetting

7 Hayley was excited because she had just one more week before she could .... on holiday.

   A get   **B** become   **C** go   **D** catch

8 Kerim .... a table for four at his favourite restaurant online.

   A commanded   **B** asked   **C** demanded   **D** booked

5 Complete each gap with a verb from Exercise 4 in the correct form. One verb is used twice.

It took me a long time to **(1)** .... to terms with the break-up of Fearnley Gold. They were my favourite band from about the age of 12 until 16. I knew everything about them and I went to see them play live half a dozen times. I remember when the lead singer **(2)** .... their intentions to break up and I just cried for days. To **(3)** .... them credit, I understand why they had to split up. They all wanted to do different things, like acting in movies, and the lead singer **(4)** .... married. But I **(5)** .... such a shock when I heard they would no longer be such a large part of my life.

Useful language Adjectives + prepositions

6 Which prepositions usually follow the adjectives below? Write *of*, *about*, *to*, *at* or *for* next to each adjective.

Remember!

Remember that some words can be followed by more than one preposition, depending on the context.

1 addicted	**2** afraid	**3** allergic ....
4 anxious	**5** ashamed	**6** enthusiastic ....
7 excited	**8** famous	**9** good ....
10 guilty	**11** married	**12** proud ....
13 similar	**14** suitable	**15** worried ....

7 Complete each sentence with a suitable adjective and preposition from Exercise 6.

1 When I was a kid I was .... the dark so I always slept with a light on in my room.

2 Everyone knows that smoking is not .... your health.

3 This area of the country is .... its amazing views.

4 My sister has to be very careful when we eat at restaurants because she is .... nuts of any kind.

5 I think I must be .... my phone. I can't go five minutes without checking it.

6 I'm .... our chances in the final. If we play our best, I think we could win.

7 You ought to be .... your attitude. That's not a kind thing to say.

8 Your group's project was very .... one I received from a different group last year. Did you copy it?

Useful language Meanings of words

8 Complete the sentences in each group using the correct words from the box. Use each word once only.

| hope | estimate | forecast | predict |

1 I .... the cost for all the work to be about £1,000.

2 If you had to .... the winner of the race, who would it be?

3 We .... to deliver the results tomorrow morning.

4 The .... for tomorrow is heavy rain and high winds.

| advise | display | indicate | recommend |

5 Can you .... a private teacher to help me improve my maths?

6 The school likes to .... all of its awards in reception for visitors to see.

7 I'd .... you to think hard before you decide what you want to study at university.

8 The research seems to .... that fewer people are driving today than in the past.

| look | scene | sight | view |

9 The .... from the hotel was amazing!

10 You should have seen the .... on his face when he found out he was on the team. He couldn't believe it!

11 I love the way the author sets the .... in the first chapter.

12 Dani laughed out loud at the .... of her friend falling off her chair in class.

| concert | music | rhythm | song |

13 When I am running, I love to listen to rock .... because it gives me more energy.

14 I have no sense of ...., so I am a terrible dancer.

15 Angelina ran to the dance floor when the DJ played her favourite ....

16 After the .... Trevor and his friends had a pizza and talked about how great the evening was.

| actually | generally | mostly | normally |

17 Trevor didn't .... want to go to the party, but all his friends persuaded him to go.

18 I wouldn't .... do this, but because you've finished your work, I'll let you leave early.

19 The doctor said my health is .... good, but I could improve it by doing more exercise.

20 After finishing school, Nina spent a year travelling, ... in Asia but also for a short while in Europe.

For questions **1–8**, read the text below and decide which answer (**A**, **B**, **C** or **D**) best fits each gap. There is an example at the beginning (**0**).

Mark your answers **on the separate answer sheet**.

Example:

0 **A** knowledgeable **B** aware **C** familiar **D** awake

0	A	B	C	D
	⊏⊐	▬	⊏⊐	⊏⊐

England National Girls' Football Week
by Amy King, 16

As most people are probably **(0)** .... , there is little doubt that football is England's most popular sport. However, most people don't realise that the number of boys and men playing the game is currently in **(1)** .... But I'm proud to say that the same is not **(2)** .... of the girls' and women's game – in fact, far from it. In April 2015, Girls' Football Week **(3)** .... no less than 22,000 girl players. Over 200 schools across England took part in the **(4)** ....

At the following Girls' Football Week in October 2016, the focus was more about **(5)** .... participation in women's football across the country's colleges and universities. Again, the event seems to have been a **(6)** .... success. At the last **(7)** .... , nearly three million girls and women were registered as football players, which is fantastic to hear. But what is the best news of all? My school has just **(8)** .... plans to set up a girls' football team next term. I will definitely be signing up!

1	**A** fall	**B** decline	**C** decrease	**D** reduction
2	**A** real	**B** right	**C** actual	**D** true
3	**A** attracted	**B** pulled	**C** engaged	**D** brought
4	**A** experience	**B** act	**C** event	**D** development
5	**A** stretching	**B** adding	**C** increasing	**D** enhancing
6	**A** great	**B** good	**C** high	**D** strong
7	**A** statistic	**B** number	**C** quantity	**D** count
8	**A** said	**B** announced	**C** told	**D** advised

In this part you:
- **read** a text with eight gaps
- **think** of a word that fills each gap correctly

Useful language Comparative and superlative phrases

Tip! This part of the test is mainly about grammar, e.g. tenses, pronouns and prepositions. There are usually a few questions on vocabulary, e.g. linking expressions, phrasal verbs and fixed phrases or expressions.

1 Complete the sentences with the words from the box.

| as | fewer | least | many | most | much | not | the |

1 .... earlier we leave, the sooner we'll get home.
2 There were not as .... people at the show as I had expected.
3 Nobody can cook .... well as my grandmother.
4 Unfortunately, your results recently have .... been as impressive as last year.
5 Well done, Sebastian! You had the .... number of absences in the last year.
6 The phone in the shop was .... more expensive than the one online.
7 According to my history teacher, Ireland is unique in Europe because there are .... people living there than in the 1840s.
8 I had one of the .... incredible days of my life when I went on holiday last year!

2 Choose the correct word in each of the sentences.
1 Are you sure you studied *as / so* hard as possible?
2 I've waited far too long already. I refuse to wait *not / any* longer.
3 I took so *many / much* risks because I was desperate to win the game.
4 Obafami had moved away from his home village when he was only five, but ten years later it looked exactly the same *as / like* before.
5 Welcome to your final, and *most / more* important, year of school.
6 Antonia was disappointed to have *fewer / less* money than she thought and so couldn't afford to go to the cinema.

Useful language Countable and uncountable nouns

3 Are the quantifiers in the box used with countable or uncountable nouns? Write the quantifiers in the appropriate columns of the table.

Tip! Your understanding of countable and uncountable nouns is often tested by asking you to think of an appropriate article (*a/an*, *the*), quantifier (e.g. *many, few*) or determiner (e.g *both, every*).

> a large amount of   a good deal of   a lot of   much   many
> plenty of   several   (a) few   (a) little   a small number of

plural countables	uncountables	plural countables and uncountables

4 Choose the correct words in the sentences.

1 How *much / many* of the children came to school today?

2 Because of the computer virus, *little / few* of the work we did yesterday has been saved.

3 There will be *a lot of / a good deal of* people in the crowd today for the football match.

4 *Several / A large amount of* restaurants have opened up in my area recently, and some of them are very good.

5 My aunt gave me *many / plenty of* good advice about what to do at university.

6 The *amount of / number of* free software I can find for my tablet is incredible! I never need to pay for anything.

7 There is *a good deal of / a large number of* work that still needs to be done on this project.

8 I have *a little / a few* coins from my holiday that the bank will not exchange for me. I suppose I'll have to keep them as souvenirs.

5 Correct these sentences.

1 Little people don't have mobile phones nowadays. ....

2 These new planes are so small that little luggages can be carried on them. ....

3 Much governments are trying to increase investment in schools. ....

4 In my opinion, pollution are going to be the biggest problem we face in the future. ....

5 The lifeguard gave us good advices about where we could and could not surf. ....

6 A large number of traffic is on the roads nowadays causing lots of congestion. ....

7 Many candidates fail the exam because they do not realise they have a few time. ....

8 I just don't understand why a large number of rainforest is being destroyed. ....

Useful language *enough, so, such, too, very*

6 Complete the sentences with the words from the box. (You do not need to use one of the words.)

enough   so   such   too   very

> **Remember!**
>
> Remember that *too* and *very* are not synonyms. The word *too* is usually negative and suggests an excess of something.

1 If you want to get into a top university, it is not .... that you have excellent grades, you must also show you have a good attitude.

2 I'm sorry, but you are .... late to join this year's language course.

3 Kieran was .... happy to get a new games console for his birthday that he spent the whole day setting it up and playing on it.

4 It was .... a good film I want to go and see it again.

5 The room just isn't big .... for so many students.

6 Electronic devices .... as phones and computers are not allowed in the examination room.

7 It's .... hot for me today so I'm going to a shopping centre where they have air conditioning.

8 There was .... a lot of snow that all the schools in the district were closed.

Useful language Prepositions

7 Complete the sentences with the appropriate prepositions.

1 Jo was so disappointed that she'd had to leave the dance contest due .... an injury.

2 When I go .... holiday, I like to just sit on the beach and do nothing.

3 It isn't safe to swim .... the water here. You should move up the river to where it is cleaner.

4 Kim hated having to be the person who always took .... the rubbish.

5 I can hardly hear the programme. Can you turn .... the volume, please?

6 Harriet was excited about going to a new school, but .... the same time, she was worried about missing her old friends.

7 Miguel put .... his birthday party for a week because he had an exam the following day.

8 I know you haven't been playing the guitar for long, but you shouldn't give .... just because something is hard.

For questions **9–16**, read the text below and think of the word which best fits each gap. Use only **one** word in each gap. There is an example at the beginning (**0**).

Write your answer **IN CAPITAL LETTERS on the separate answer sheet**.

Example: | **0** | | H | A | D | | | | | | | | | | | | | | | | | | |

Manatees

I have to admit that until I went to Florida in the USA, I don't think I **(0)** .... ever heard of manatees. They are large mammals which live in sea water and are also known **(9)** .... 'sea cows'. This is partly due **(10)** .... their cow-like appearance, and also because of their diet. They are vegetarians who live **(11)** .... weeds and grass that they find under water. In fact, they can eat as **(12)** .... as 50 kg of this in a day. The adult manatees weigh up to 590 kg.

Manatee populations have been suffering recently; in fact conservationists were **(13)** .... concerned that they have declared the manatee an endangered species. When I went to see these animals in the wild, **(14)** .... amazed me was their appearance. Their lips have left and right sides, which can move independently of **(15)** .... another. Manatees are slow and graceful in the water, which, **(16)** .... me, was an incredible sight to see.

In this part you:

- **read**   a text with eight gaps
- **form**   an appropriate word for each gap from the word in capital letters
          at the end of the line

Useful language Suffixes

1 Which kind of word (adjective, adverb, noun or verb) is needed to fill in
the gaps in these sentences?

  1 Wow! That has to be the most delicious .... I have ever
  eaten in my life.

  2 That was such an .... difficult test!

  3 I suddenly .... that I was going to have a few problems
  getting out of the stadium.

  4 The key to a .... relationship is being open and honest with
  each other.

2 Add suffixes from the box to the words below to make nouns. You may
need to make some spelling changes.

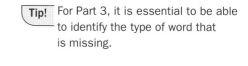

Tip! For Part 3, it is essential to be able to identify the type of word that is missing.

-al	-ing	-ion/-tion	-ism	-ity	-ment	-ness	-ship

  1 lazy   **2** pay   **3** tour   **4** similar

  5 greet   **6** decorate   **7** partner   **8** able

  9 govern   **10** relation   **11** argue   **12** approve

3 Add suffixes from the box to the words below to make verbs. You may
need to make some spelling changes.

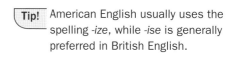

Tip! American English usually uses the spelling -ize, while -ise is generally preferred in British English.

-ate	-en	-ify	-ise

  1 hard   **2** clear   **3** economy   **4** active

  5 sympathy   **6** short   **7** identity   **8** final

4 Add suffixes from the box to the words below to make adjectives. You
may need to make some spelling changes.

-able	-al	-ful	-ing	-ive	-ous	-y

  1 fun   **2** memory   **3** peace   **4** accident

  5 consider   **6** disaster   **7** distinct   **8** promise

  9 extend   **10** expense   **11** addict   **12** magic

5 **Write the adverb form(s) for each of these words.**

1 hard	**2** regular	**3** peace	**4** terrible
5 hungry	**6** good	**7** easy	**8** increase

Tip! Not all word changes are simply formed by adding a suffix.

6 **Change these words to nouns.**

1 choose	**2** true	**3** weigh	**4** live
5 fly	**6** hot	**7** long	**8** prove
9 succeed	**10** grow	**11** high	**12** die

7 **Complete the sentences with the correct forms of the words from the box.**

Tip! Begin by trying to identify the type of word that is missing.

> calm   cruel   real   fame   homeless   short   surprise   amaze

1 .... against animals must be one of the worst things humans are capable of.

2 The issue of .... seems to be on the increase. The government should prioritise finding these people a place to live.

3 There were .... few people at the game. Considering it was the final, I would have expected more to turn up.

4 They had to .... the film because originally it was nearly four hours long.

5 I went to a music festival last year and there were .... people everywhere. There were actors, singers and even some politicians.

6 I was quite nervous, to be honest, but to everyone's .... the food that Sylvie cooked was very tasty!

7 It's lovely to see you! I didn't .... that you had been invited to this party as well.

8 In case of a fire, walk .... to your nearest exit.

For questions **17–24**, read the text below. Use the word given in capitals at the end of some of the lines to form a word that fits in the gap **in the same line**. There is an example at the beginning (0).

Write your answer **IN CAPITAL LETTERS on the separate answer sheet**.

Example: | 0 | I | N | I | T | I | A | L | L | Y | | | | | | | | |

My 16th birthday

I turned 16 last week. And I have to say that **(0)** .... , I didn't   **INITIAL**

enjoy my birthday much. I usually get some birthday **(17)** ....   **GREET**

from my friends on social media. But nobody wished me a happy birthday,

which was a bit **(18)** ....   **DEPRESS**

After school, I noticed that the friends I usually walk home with had all

(19) .... , so I walked back alone. But then when I got back   **APPEAR**

to my house, there were lots of **(20)** .... and balloons on the   **DECORATE**

outside. 'OK,' I thought, 'this looks more **(21)** ....' So I went   **PROMISE**

inside, and there, waiting in the sitting room, were all of my school friends!

Seeing them there was so **(22)** .... ! Together with my parents,   **EXPECT**

they'd arranged this surprise party. And they'd done it all without my

(23) .... ! In fact, it was probably the most special and   **KNOW**

(24) .... party ever!   **MEMORY**

In this part you:

- **read**   six sentences
- **rewrite**   the sentences using the word in capital letters so that your answers have a similar meaning

Useful language Three-part phrasal verbs

1   Match the phrasal verbs 1–8 with the definitions a–h. Use a dictionary if necessary.

1	look forward to	**a**	accept a difficult situation or person
2	look up to	**b**	feel excited about something that is going to happen
3	get away with	**c**	finish or use all of something
4	come up with	**d**	think of an idea or plan
5	cut down on	**e**	admire and respect someone
6	run out of	**f**	defend or support a person or idea
7	stand up for	**g**	succeed in avoiding punishment
8	put up with	**h**	do or use less of something

2   Read the email below about holiday plans. Complete the text with the correct forms of the phrasal verbs from Exercise 1.

Hi Eric,

I'm really **(1)** .... you staying at my place for the holiday. It's going to be great and I'm sure you'll love my new friends. Tell me what time your train arrives and I'll get Dad to meet you.

I've **(2)** .... a few ideas for things we can do while you're here. There's a great new water park outside town that I know you are going to love. I think you're also going to like the new cinema near me. There are loads of other things to do, but you'll have time to decide what you want to do when you get here.

Unfortunately, we'll have to look after my younger sister while my mum and dad are at work. She can be a bit annoying at times, but it's only for the afternoons so we'll just have to **(3)** .... her.

Let me know if there's anything you need. Last time we met you were trying to **(4)** .... how much meat you eat. Are you still doing that? I'll have to tell my mum to get some vegetarian food for you if you are.

Speak soon!

Omar

Useful language Modal verbs

3 Look at the sentences about the information in the email in Exercise 2. Complete with phrases from the box.

| might have become | must live | can't have seen | may be studying | can choose | can't be |

1 Eric and Omar .... in different places.
2 Eric .... film at college.
3 Eric .... what he wants to do when he visits Omar.
4 Omar .... the youngest child in the family.
5 Eric .... a vegetarian.
6 Eric and Omar .... each other for some time because Omar doesn't know what Eric likes to eat.

4 Which sentence in Exercise 3 talks about something that:

1 was impossible? ....
2 is possible? ....
3 is almost certain? ....
4 is impossible? ....
5 was possible? ....
6 is allowed? ....

Useful language *-ing* and *to* + infinitive

5 Choose the correct word in each sentence.

1 After six months of intensive study, Fadela's maths grades finally appeared *being / to be* improving.
2 I don't appreciate *having / to have* my younger brother sleeping in my room.
3 Dad's car needs *fixing / to fix* so I have to walk to school this week.
4 Thomas learnt *speaking / to speak* Japanese when he was a child because he lived in Japan for two years.
5 Louisa really didn't feel like *doing / to do* her homework, but she knew she had to.
6 I avoid *shopping / to shop* on Saturdays because everything is just so busy.
7 Do you agree *telling / to tell* the truth?
8 Haruki's aunt offered *give / to give* him her old games console.

For questions **25–30**, complete the second sentence so that it has a similar meaning to the first sentence, using the word given. **Do not change the word given.** You must use between **two** and **five** words, including the word given. Here is an example (0).

Example:

0   I haven't seen you for ages!

TIME

It has .... I saw you!

The gap can be filled by the words 'been a long time since', so you write:

Example: | 0 | BEEN A LONG TIME SINCE |

Write **only** the missing words **IN CAPITAL LETTERS on the separate answer sheet**.

---

25   Jane thought of a name for her new band.
CAME
Jane .... a name for her new band.

26   It took me ages to get to sleep.
ASLEEP
I didn't .... ages.

27   Perhaps Alessio missed his bus.
HAVE
Alessio .... caught his bus.

28   I have to charge my phone each day.
CHARGING
My phone .... a day.

29   I went to bed late because it took me ages to do my homework.
TIME
I spent so .... my homework that I went to bed late.

30   Dan and his brother are both wearing identical shirts.
ON
Dan has the .... his brother.

In this part you:

- **read**   a long text
- **answer**   six multiple-choice questions
- **choose**   your answer from four options (**A**, **B**, **C** and **D**)

1   Read quickly through the text about a teenager competing in a high jump competition. Then cover your text and in pairs see how much you can remember about the text.

> **Tip!** There will probably be some words in the text that you don't know. It's possible to complete this task without understanding every word.

Flying through the air

Hisanori was on his own now. He was standing on the side of the track waiting for his first jump of the competition. Indeed, it would be his first competitive jump in over six months. As he stood waiting, he reflected on his life over the past half year and how <u>it</u> had changed so much. When he had won the under-16s national championships he had been so happy and excited. All those long hours of training after school and at weekends had paid off.

And then, just a couple of weeks after the greatest day of his life <u>it</u> had happened. He had been riding home on his bike after training when he crashed and broke his leg. The pain in his leg was not as bad as the agony of not being able to train and compete. He had been able to catch up on his school work, which his school appreciated, but it was not something he was especially proud of. He missed the physical activity of training and the adrenaline rush of competing. His friends and family had rallied around and tried to keep the negative feelings away, but <u>they</u> could not really understand.

But all of <u>that</u> was over. All the hard work in getting back to fitness would soon be rewarded. The opportunity to fly through the air made everything worthwhile.

---

2   Read through the text again. How does Hisanori feel?

3   Read the four options below. Which one is closest to your answer in Exercise 2?

> **Tip!** There is often a question that tests your understanding of the whole text. There isn't one word or sentence in the text that will give you the answer.

   A   Sad because of the training he has missed due to his injury.

   B   Happy that he was able to do more school work.

   C   Satisfied that, despite the problems he has faced, he is ready to jump again.

   D   Nervous to be competing again.

4   Look at the underlined words in the text in Exercise 1 and choose the correct options in the following questions.

 Tip! Pronouns such as *it*, *this*, *one* and *their* refer to other words and phrases. Usually they refer to information which comes earlier in the text, but they can also refer to information which is still to come, as in question 2.

   1   In the first paragraph, *it* refers to

   A   Hisanori's life

   B   the past six months

   C   the competition

   2   In the first sentence of the second paragraph, *it* refers to

   A   the school

   B   the accident

   C   catching up on school work

   3   At the end of the second paragraph, *they* refers to

   A   negative feelings

   B   friends and family

   C   weights

   4   In the final paragraph, *that* refers to

   A   his friends and family not understanding

   B   doing his homework

   C   the problems associated with breaking his leg

5   Read the final paragraph of the text. How does Hisanori feel about the jump? Underline the parts of the text which reveal his feelings.

And then, as quick as a flash it was all over. Initially, relief flooded through him as he realised his first jump was a successful one. He punched the air in delight and was almost as happy as the time he won the national championships. He ran back to his coach with a large smile on his face. But even before he got back, he started thinking about the next jump and how he could improve. He knew he could get better and jump higher. He tried to ignore the fact that he was so happy and focus on how to improve, how to get better. He realised his sport was the search for perfection and it was this search that he had missed so much when he had been recovering from injury.

6   Which sentence best summarises Hisanori's true feelings towards his sport?

   A   Hisanori is relieved that he can jump again.

   B   Hisanori enjoys trying to get better and better.

   C   Hisanori feels that his next jump will always be a better jump.

   D   Hisanori is worried he might get injured again.

You are going to read an article about a list of books for teenage readers. For questions **31–36**, choose the answer (**A**, **B**, **C** or **D**) which you think fits best according to the text.

Mark your answers **on the separate answer sheet**.

World Book Day – the best teen reads

by Genny Haslett, 24, English literature teacher at Bathampton Secondary School

It is often suggested that teachers and librarians aren't pushing secondary school readers towards titles that challenge them enough, and so the organisers of World Book Day have announced a list which might provide some inspiration for anyone who's stuck for ideas. This list of popular books for young adults, voted for by 10,000 people across the UK, features a top 10 to 'shape and inspire' teenagers, and handle some of the challenges of adolescence.

All but one of the books have already been made into films, demonstrating that when a book makes it to the big screen, it often then acquires more readers thanks to the film's success. Of course, this isn't always the case, as with George Orwell's *1984*, where the rather mediocre film does not compare so favourably with the book's ability to conjure up a dark vision of life in a police state.

James Bowen's *A Streetcat Named Bob*, published in 2012, is one of the few relatively contemporary books here. It's also certainly for me the least predictable member of the list, but its extended stay on the bestseller list earned it – and its author – a devoted following. It is the touching story of Bob, the cat who helped a homeless man called James get his life back on track. Bob sits on James's shoulder and sleeps at his feet while he plays the guitar on the street, and soon becomes the centre of attention. What makes the story particularly powerful is that it is based on author James Bowen's real life.

Also on the list are J. K. Rowling's *Harry Potter* books. In this case it's actually the whole series rather than one particular title that makes the shortlist. Perhaps the judges struggled to agree which one book to pick. For me, the books are rather more pre-teen than the rest of the books on the list, which are aimed at a more mature readership.

But Harry Potter is a special case: as Harry gets older in each successive book in the series, the stories do become more complex and darker. In a way, readers themselves grow up with Harry and his friends. Rowling asks some tough questions about standing up to authority, challenging 'normal' views and many other subjects close to teenage readers' hearts. This should get rid of the idea that the whole series is just for young kids. In actual fact, half of all *Harry Potter* readers are over the age of 35, but that's another story.

The list goes right back to the nineteenth century with Charlotte Brontë's great romance *Jane Eyre*, showing that some books never grow old, though the majority are twentieth-century works such as Anne Frank's heartbreaking wartime memoir *The Diary of a Young Girl*, which even now I find hard to get through without shedding tears. Personally, I would have swapped J. R. R. Tolkien's *The Lord of the Rings* for one of the many classics that didn't make the final selection, *Lord of the Flies* perhaps, William Golding's nightmare vision of schoolboys stuck on an island.

Of course there'll always be some choices we don't agree with, but that's what I think makes a list like this so fascinating. I've been using it with my class of 16-year-olds, and I got them to evaluate it and make other suggestions for what to include or how it could be changed. But what I hope can really make a lasting difference is if it stimulates them to try out writers on the list, perhaps ones they haven't come across before, and be introduced to new styles of writing.

31 What criticism does the writer make in the first paragraph?

    A   World Book Day has been poorly organised.

    B   School librarians aren't working hard enough.

    C   Teenagers are reading books that are too easy.

    D   Teachers don't encourage pupils to read enough.

32 What point is made about books which are made into films?

    A   The best books tend to be made into films.

    B   The film of a book makes more people read the book.

    C   Many people prefer to watch a film than read the book.

    D   It is useful to be able to compare the book and the film.

33 What does the writer suggest about *A Streetcat Named Bob*?

    A   She is surprised that it is on the list.

    B   The book did not sell as well as it deserved to.

    C   It is the most recently published book on the list.

    D   It is the only autobiography on the list.

34 How does the writer justify the presence of the *Harry Potter* books on the list?

    A   The books' fame can help the list get more attention.

    B   The later books in the series are more suitable for teenagers.

    C   Teenagers should read books that they will also enjoy as adults.

    D   It makes sense to have a whole series as well as individual books.

35 Which book does the writer feel shouldn't be on the list?

    A   *Jane Eyre*

    B   *The Diary of a Young Girl*

    C   *The Lord of the Rings*

    D   *Lord of the Flies*

36 What does the writer intend to do?

    A   be more fully developed in future

    B   prompt pupils to read more widely

    C   enable pupils to write more effectively

    D   provide a useful topic for discussion in class

In this part you:

- **read**   a text with six sentences missing
- **choose**   the correct sentence to fit each gap

Useful language Synonyms

1 Find two synonyms from the box for each of these words. Write the synonyms on the lines.

> **Tip!** Synonyms are often used in the same sentence or paragraph and can help you identify the correct answer.

allow	approve	attentive	dependable
dusk	infant	nightfall	thoughtful
trustworthy	youngster		

1 agree .... , ...

2 child .... , ...

3 considerate .... , ...

4 evening .... , ...

5 reliable .... , ...

Useful language Purpose, reason and result

2 Look at the underlined phrases in the sentences below. Decide whether each phrase introduces a purpose, a reason or a result.

1 I was checking my results online <u>just in case</u> I had to do any of the exams again. ....REASON.......

2 Gustavo forgot his keys <u>so</u> he had to get his brother to let me in the house. ....

3 I was told that <u>because</u> the computers weren't working, I would have to come back the following day. ....

4 I save half my pocket money every month <u>so as to</u> have some extra for my holidays. ....

5 <u>Since</u> the end-of-year concert is coming up, I am having extra piano lessons. ....

6 Amy had to wear headphones <u>so that</u> she wouldn't wake the baby. ....

3 Join the sentences using the words in brackets and making any other changes that are necessary.

1 Many schools want their students to wear school uniform. They want their students to feel part of a community. (**so that**)

2 It's a good idea to do homework as soon as you get it. You might have a problem later and not be able to finish your homework in time. (**just in case**)

3 Gina chose to wear make-up. She wanted to look older. (**so as to**)

4 You have to wake up early tomorrow. You should go to bed now. (**since**)

5 Super A can charge a lot of money for its phones. Many people believe Super A produces the best phones. (**so**)

6 I think you're going to be very successful. You've done a lot of hard work to prepare for the exam. (**because**)

You are going to read an article about an unusual school in Germany, where the pupils have a great deal of freedom. Six sentences have been removed from the article. Choose from the sentences **A–G** the one which fits each gap (**37–42**). There is one extra sentence which you do not need to use.

Mark your answers **on the separate answer sheet**.

Open-air teaching In Germany
A bold experiment in education that aims to help young students become independent thinkers

In 2013, Wolfgang Schwarz became Assistant Headteacher at a Hamburg school. It was a conventional school: teachers taught lessons that pupils had to attend, and set compulsory homework for pupils. The school taught all the usual subjects from English to maths. The Senior Management team told the teachers what to do, and the teachers told the pupils what to do.

Shortly after this, Schwarz read an article about open-air schools, whose aim is to encourage children to be more independent and develop important life skills in a natural setting. **37** This is in contrast to more traditional schools like where Schwarz was working, where (according to critics) the focus is too much on the teaching and learning of factual information, and where children aren't given enough opportunity to learn how to think for themselves. They maintain that the physical limitations of the classroom stop students learning naturally. Learning outside, in a forest or on a beach encourages students to think more about the world around them.

However, there were only a small number of outdoor schools across Germany. **38** In 2014, that is exactly what he did, and the Hamburg Outdoor School was born. With four teachers and 42 children aged between 4 and 18, Schwarz's school had a small building set in large grounds near a beach and private forest. Now they use the areas outside the school more than the old classrooms. Most lessons take place outside.

What actually makes it an 'outdoor' school? How does it work in practice? **39** There are no tests and no homework you have to do, although some parents have, additionally, set their children academic tasks to complete away from school.

The curriculum is certainly not conventional. **40** Last year, the students sampled more than 80 different subjects, learning some maths, history and physics in the process.

And some of the teaching is done by the students themselves, such as a course on geology, taught by 13-year-old Dieter Altmann, which has become one of the most popular at the school. Other subjects range from juggling to fishing techniques.

However, student independence isn't just limited as to how the children actually do their learning. **41** At these sessions, anything can be discussed, ranging from discipline issues to deciding who should be allowed to start at the school. Everyone, from the youngest child to the school Headteacher, has an equal vote in all this. All decisions are made democratically, so the teachers can be outvoted by the children theoretically; this is something which does happen from time to time. The key question is this: does a school with optional lessons and student-led courses on juggling really provide students with the best start in life? **42** Accepting that students in normal schools may become better at certain skills, he maintains that children can learn facts much better in a natural environment through experimentation and observation. 'If you learn out of the classroom in the natural world, it makes learning more meaningful and memorable'.

A   Schwarz is convinced that it can.

B   But Schwarz never saw this as a problem.

C   These include critical thinking and the ability to socialise.

D   Simple: the children make the rules, choose their classes and where to work.

E   They basically run the school too, through their weekly discussion meetings.

F   So this got Schwarz thinking: why not open one himself?

G   The pupils study rare crafts like soap-making, and Mr Schwarz has even taught classes in cheese-tasting.

In this part you:

- **read** through one long text divided into sections, or up to six shorter texts
- **find** information in the text that matches ten short questions

1 Read through the text quickly and answer the questions.

   1 What is the text about?

   2 Where might you see it?

   3 Is it positive or negative?

> **Tip!** You don't have to read the text in detail to find the answers to these questions. Skimming is a reading strategy that will help you in the exam.

Zhang Woo ★★★★

I liked this game because it was something I could do to pass the time and it's fun if you want something cute. I enjoyed it, but after playing for a long period of time it can become a bit boring. I would give it five stars if it had more variety in the challenges. The graphics are pretty good and the music is nice too. All in all, though, for a free game it is very good.

---

2 Read the two texts quickly and answer the questions below.

Karima Abdulaziz ★★★★★

I love all games of this type, but this is the best one around. It's really challenging and you have to think very hard to complete all of the levels. I always play on silent so I don't know what the music is like, but the visual effects are amazing. I like the social aspect as well as I can invite my friends to help me when I have a problem. The only thing I would add is an option to pay for the game so that I could avoid the adverts.

Pawel Kiminski ★★★

It's an interesting game, but it quickly becomes repetitive. Once you have learnt how to complete the first few levels, it is easy to do the rest of them. The artwork is very well done, but the music is annoying – I had it on silent all of the time. The adverts are a bit frustrating and not exactly appropriate if children are playing. However, there were no bugs and the gameplay is very good and, at the end of the day, it is free so I can't complain too much!

Which writer (Zhang, Karima or Pawel)

1 would like to pay for the game?

2 doesn't like the music?

3 makes a recommendation for change?

4 thinks it can be difficult at times?

5 believes there might be a problem for younger people?

You are going to read an article about four teenagers who have started their own business. For questions **43–52**, choose from the teenagers (**A–D**). The teenagers may be chosen more than once.

Mark your answers **on the separate answer sheet**.

Which teenager

says they are highly motivated?	**43**	
has started to feel more confident?	**44**	
is planning to open another business?	**45**	
says that managing time can be hard?	**46**	
says they learn from their mistakes?	**47**	
says that their age surprises some people?	**48**	
tends not to tell people how old they are?	**49**	
wanted to improve an experience for customers?	**50**	
says their work involves something they find easy?	**51**	
realised what they wanted to do while helping someone else?	**52**	

Four teenage business stars

A Rebecca Dundee, 16

I suppose it was obvious I had a head for business when I was about six. I used to make my parents cups of tea in the morning – and charge them 20p for each one. And it was another 20p if it needed reheating. And then about a year ago I was in a chain coffee shop waiting in line to get my drink, and I just realised how dreadful the whole experience was – dirty tables, rubbish WiFi and grumpy staff. And I thought 'I bet I could do better than that'. So a friend and I launched an app enabling people to access menus, order and interact with each other. Since then I haven't looked back. I was concerned that I wasn't doing too well at school, which was a bit depressing, but with the business going so well, it feels great to be where I am now.

B Jimbo, 15

When people ask what I do, I tell them I advise people about their brand on social media. They can't believe I'm doing this while I'm so young. But I love it. The tricky bit is getting everything done that I need to; sometimes there aren't enough hours in the day! I've been doing the job about six months, and it took quite a lot of effort at the start to persuade my mum and dad that it wasn't just a waste of time. But now they're confident I'm doing OK. Which is just as well, because now that I've launched an online magazine, I should have several more projects on the way, as long as I can get the money together. One's going to be setting up a firm with my best mate – it should start to do quite well after about a year. So watch this space!

C Sarah McFinny, 18

Using social media comes naturally to me, and it's not something I've ever had to try to get my head around. I'm in my first year at uni, and I was lending a hand to someone who wanted to organise a social media campaign for a university sports club. I did lots of work for her, setting it up and publicising it, and she couldn't believe the results I got. It was amazing! So I thought, 'You know what – I could make some money out of doing this sort of thing'. When I'm talking to clients, obviously I don't shout about my age, I mean you want to be taken seriously. When I graduate, I want to help my parents run their business, or at least do that part-time. I'm excited about the future.

D Duncan Jackson, 15

Well, I've never liked spending money, even at a really young age. But now that I've worked out how to make money, I'm really driven to get out of bed every morning and make as much as I can. I basically run an online shop, and I've had over 100 customers so far. It's always nice when a customer visits the store and buys from you again – you know you're doing something right. I don't always get things right though. In fact, there are lots of things I've got very wrong, like setting my prices too high – or too low! But that can be useful, because when something doesn't go as planned, you can always adapt and hope you do it better next time.

In this part you:

- **read**   the instructions and the essay question carefully
- **read**   the notes that you must include in your essay
- **write**   a formal essay that gives your opinion
- **include**   the points you need to cover, and add another point of your own
- **write**   between 140 and 190 words

1a Read the instructions for a Part 1 essay task. Underline the key words in the instructions.

> In your English class you have been talking about the importance of physical exercise and sport for young people. Now your English teacher has asked you to write an essay.

b How much exercise do you get? Discuss in pairs. Think about the following situations:

- at school
- on the way to school
- sports and hobbies
- physical work, (e.g. cleaning, carrying things)

2 The phrases in the box can be used for talking about the benefits of physical exercise and sport. Find phrases from the box that match the definitions. Write them on the lines.

> **Tip!** As part of your essay planning, brainstorm a list of high-level words about the topic. You can then choose which words from your list you want to include in your writing.

energy	leadership skills	physical strength
posture	risk of heart disease	risk of obesity
self-confidence	stamina	strength of character
stress level	teamwork skills	well-being

1 how long you can continue exercise before getting tired ....

2 the way you sit or stand ....

3 a positive feeling about your own abilities ....

4 the danger of becoming dangerously overweight ....

Useful language Verbs

3a Look at the verbs in the box. Check any new words in a dictionary.

boost	build up	develop	improve	increase
lower	raise	reduce	strengthen	weaken

b Group the verbs according to meaning. Some verbs can go in more than one group.

1 make better / stronger ....

2 make bigger / higher ....

3 make smaller / weaker ....

c Write sentences about physical exercise. Use the verbs and phrases from this page to help you.

Example   *Physical exercise can boost your self-confidence.*

4a Look again at the instructions for the Part 1 essay task in Exercise 1.
Now read the essay question and the notes below.

> **'School students spend too much time on sports. They should spend
> more time studying instead.' Do you agree?**
>
> **Notes**
>
> Write about:
>
>   1. health benefits and risks of doing sport
>
>   2. how sports affect the way you study
>
>   3. .... (your own idea)
>
> Write an essay using **all** the notes and giving reasons for your point of view.

b Before you decide whether you agree with the statement, complete the list below with some points that you
could make in your essay.

- health **benefits** of sports
- health **risks** of sports
- How do sports **help** you to study?
- How do sports **make it harder** to study?

c As well as the two points provided in the essay question, you must also write about a third point. Look at five
ideas for the third point and answer questions 1–3 below.

   a Physical exercise is fun and rewarding.

   b Students need to simply relax after school, e.g. watch TV, chat with friends, listen to music.

   c Sports teach useful skills and habits for life.

   d More time studying means better test results and grades.

   e Sports are not fair: students who are good at sports always win.

   1 Which points support the statement in the essay question?

   2 Which points challenge the statement?

   3 Which points are not relevant to this essay task?

5 Decide whether you will agree or disagree with the statement in the
question. Which of the points in Exercise 4 would you include in your
essay? Would you include any different points?

> **Tip!** The essay doesn't have to reflect
> your own personal opinion. It's
> usually possible to think of good
> arguments from each side. You
> can choose the opinion that allows
> you to display your knowledge of
> grammar and vocabulary best.

6 Now read what a student called Martin wrote in answer to the essay task. Does he agree or disagree with the statement?

Some people argue that schools should focus only on academic subjects, like mathematics and history. But I believe that physical exercise is just as important as any other subject.

The health benefits of physical exercise are clear. It improves our posture, boosts our physical strength and lowers our risk of heart disease and obesity. For some students, PE lessons are the only physical exercise that they get each week, so every lesson makes a big difference to their health.

Physical exercise actually helps us to study. It reduces our stress levels and increases our energy. After doing physical exercise, we feel fresh and ready to return to our studies.

In addition, sports teach us important skills that we can use in the real world. They encourage teamwork and leadership skills and also give us the stamina and strength of character to keep going when we want to give up. It makes sense for schools to develop these essential skills.

I strongly believe that physical exercise at school is not a waste of time. It definitely deserves its place in the school timetable.

Useful language Paragraphs

7a Look at Martin's essay in Exercise 6. What is the purpose of each paragraph? How many sentences are in each paragraph?

b Look at Martin's second paragraph. The first sentence makes a point. The second sentence provides examples and/or explanations. The third sentence shows how this information is linked to the essay question. Now look at Martin's third and fourth paragraphs. Do they follow the same pattern?

Tip! You shouldn't write more than 190 words. That means you'll probably need only two or three sentences in each paragraph.

8a Another student, Helena, has written an essay on the same topic. Read her essay plan.
- Paragraph 1: Introduction: agree with statement
- Paragraph 2: Health issues
- Paragraph 3: How sports affect the way you study
- Paragraph 4: Time: more time studying means better test results and grades
- Paragraph 5: Conclusion

b Now put these sentences from Helena's second, third and fourth paragraphs in the best order.

a Too much physical activity can be bad for our health. `1`

b As I have no intention of becoming a professional athlete, every hour that I spend in a PE lesson is one hour less that I can spend on more important subjects. `____`

c To make it easier to pay attention during lessons, schools should reduce the amount of physical activity that students are expected to do. `____`

d For all these reasons, we should cut sports lessons to no more than one hour per week. `____`

e For example, school students often suffer from broken bones or other injuries. `____`

f For me, the whole point of school is to study academic subjects that will help me in my future education and career. `7`

g Because they are so physically and mentally tiring, we have less energy to concentrate during lessons. `____`

h As a result, they may miss school for weeks or even months. `____`

i Sports may also make it harder for students to focus on important subjects like maths and history. `4`

You **must** answer this question. Write your answer in **140–190** words in an appropriate style **on the separate answer sheet**.

In your English class you have been talking about different kinds of sport. Now your English teacher has asked you to write an essay.

Write an essay using **all** the notes and giving reasons for your point of view.

'It is better for young people to take part in team sports at school than to practise individual sports (e.g. tennis, gymnastics).' Do you agree?

Notes

Write about:

1. enjoying the activity

2. learning to be responsible

3. .... (your own idea)

Check! Have you:

- [ ] included everything in the notes?
- [ ] written about your own idea?
- [ ] given reasons for your point of view?
- [ ] written 140–190 words?

In Part 2, you can choose what to write from a set of four options:
a letter or email, a story, an article or a review.

In a letter or email, you need to:

- **read** — part of a letter or email from a friend
- **think** — about what advice or information your friend needs
- **imagine** — that you are writing to a real person, not just answering an exam question
- **write** — between 140 and 190 words

1 You will often need to give opinions or advice as part of the letter/email task. Look at the extracts from emails below. Underline the parts of each extract where the writer justifies an opinion or piece of advice.

1 I think it's much better to read a book before you watch a film because you'll understand a lot more of the story. If you watch a film first and then read the book, you might get bored.

2 You shouldn't spend so much time playing computer games. It's bad for your health to spend so much time sitting inside. Why don't you take up a new hobby?

3 We have six 60-minute lessons every day, with a 5-minute break between each lesson and a break of 30 minutes for lunch. I think the breaks are too short – we don't have enough time to get from one lesson to the next.

4 If I were you, I wouldn't invite too many people to the party. I think it'll feel more personal if you invite only a few of your best friends, because you'll have more time to talk to each of them.

> **Tip!** In your letter or email, you may need to do any of the following things:
> - give advice
> - make a comparison
> - describe something
> - explain something
> - express your opinion
> - make a recommendation

2a Look at the exam task below.

You have received this email from your English-speaking friend, Paula.

> Hi!
>
> I like living in our new house and my new school's fine. But I don't really have any good friends. All the other people in my class already know each other well, so it's hard for me to make friends. My parents say I should join a club or something, but I'm not sure I want to.
>
> What do you think?
>
> Paula

Write your **email.**

> **Tip!** In the writing tasks, always justify your opinions and any advice which you give.

b Work with a partner. Discuss what advice you would give Paula. How could you justify your advice?

3a Read the email that a student wrote to Paula.

> Hi Paula
>
> It's great to hear from you. I'm pleased you like your new home. Sorry I haven't replied sooner, but I've been really busy.
>
> It must be really difficult to make new friends. But it'll get easier over the next few months. Maybe you should invite some classmates to your house after school. That's a great way of getting to know people better.
>
> I think your parents are right about joining a club. It's really important to spend time with people who aren't in your class. I know you don't like sports, but there are lots of other clubs you can join. I remember you love painting, so why don't you join an art class? That way, you can make friends while learning a useful skill. Or what about a dance class? It's a great way to meet new friends and keep fit at the same time. It'll feel strange at first, going to a class by yourself, but it'll be worth it.
>
> Anyway, let me know what you decide. I'm sure you'll be fine!
>
> Good luck!
>
> Antonio

b Discuss with a partner. What is the purpose of the four main paragraphs?

4a Look at this sentence from Antonio's letter. Why do you think Antonio included it?

Sorry I haven't replied sooner, but I've been really busy.

b Find a sentence in the third paragraph where Antonio invents information to make the email feel more real.

5 Match the sentences from Antonio's email with the advice.

1 It's great to hear from you.

2 It must be really difficult.

3 Anyway, let me know what you decide.

4 I'm sure you'll be fine!

a A positive prediction is a great way to end your email.

b Don't forget to invite the other person to reply.

c Always acknowledge the other person's email at the beginning.

d Show that you understand the other person's problem.

> **Tip!** Always start your letter or email with a friendly introduction and finish with a friendly ending. There's very little difference between a letter and an email. You can write them both in exactly the same way.

6a Read this extract from an email from a student called Marek.

> We've finally finished school for the summer, which is great. It was a very hard year. But now I've got a new problem: how to fill six weeks of holiday without spending loads of money. Any ideas?

b Work in pairs. Use these phrases to give advice to Marek.

- I'm pleased to hear …
- I know what you mean about …
- Maybe you should …
- That's a great way of …
- It's really important to …
- Why don't you …?
- That way, you can …
- What about …?
- It's a great way to …

Useful language Dummy subjects (*it* and *there*)

7a Find sentences in Antonio's email that mean the same as sentences a and b. Why are Antonio's versions better?

    a Spending time with people who aren't in your class is really important.

    b I know you don't like sports, but you can join lots of other clubs.

b A dummy subject is a grammatical word that functions as the subject of a sentence. There are two dummy subjects in English, *it* and *there*. Rewrite the following sentences using either *it* or *there* to start the sentence.

> **Tip!** The dummy subject doesn't mean anything by itself, but it allows us to move important information away from the beginning of a sentence.

    1 Making friends in a new school can be very difficult.

    It ....

    2 You can do lots of different things to keep busy over the summer.

    There ....

    3 Two ways of solving this problem exist.

    ....

    4 Inviting some friends round after school is a good idea.

    ....

    5 Some people you'll really like might be in your dance class.

    ....

Test 1 Exam practice   Writing • Part 2 (letter/email)

Write your answer in **140–190** words in an appropriate style **on the separate answer sheet**.

You have received this email from your English-speaking friend, Jo.

> Hi!
>
> I have to do my homework every day as soon as I get home. I want to do things like see my friends and relax straight after school – then do my homework later. But my parents don't let me do anything else until I've finished my homework. How can I persuade my parents to change their minds?
>
> Hope you can help!

> **Tip!** You don't need to answer Jo's question. If you agree with Jo's parents, and don't think they should change their minds, you can explain why in your email.

Check! Have you:

- [ ] responded to Jo's request?
- [ ] justified your opinions or advice?
- [ ] opened and closed the letter in a suitable way?
- [ ] written 140–190 words?

In Part 2, there may be a question asking you to write a short story.
In a story, you:

- **continue**   your story from the prompt sentence you are given
- **include**   the words or ideas you are given in the prompts
- **show**   that you can use a good range of past tenses
- **use**   a wide range of vocabulary to describe people, things and events
- **write**   between 140 and 190 words

1a Read the exam task below carefully.

Your teacher has asked you to write a story for a class story competition.

Your story must **begin** with this sentence:

When Angela saw the message on her phone, she ran out of the room.

Your story must include:

- an animal   • a mistake

Write your **story**.

b Use your imagination to plan the story. Think about these questions.

1 Who is Angela? What sort of room was Angela in? Why was she there?

2 Who was the message from? What did it say? How did it make her feel?

3 Was the message about an animal? What sort of animal?

4 Did the mistake happen before Angela read the message or after?

> **Tip!** It's useful to think about lots of details while you're planning. This will help your story to feel realistic. You can always leave out some details when you're writing.

2a Read part of a story that a student called Erik wrote for this task. Which questions from Exercise 1b has he answered?

SNAKES IN THE KITCHEN

When Angela saw the message on her phone, she ran out of the room. She had been watching a film at her friend's house.

'I've just had a message from my dad,' she explained to her friend. 'He said there are snakes in the kitchen. I need to help him!'

When she opened the door, she saw her dad lying on the sofa.

'Are you OK, Dad?' she called.

'Yes, absolutely fine,' replied her dad.

'But what happened to the snakes in the kitchen?' asked Angela.

'Snakes!' exclaimed her dad. 'I meant snacks! My phone must have changed my spelling!'

2b The story has only 98 words. Look at the extra information that Erik added to his story later. Where did he put the sentences in the story?

> **Tip!** Add extra information to make your story more interesting. You're allowed up to 190 words, so try to use them!

1 She knew she needed to get home as quickly as possible.

2 He told me to come home immediately.

3 As she was running home, she wondered where the snakes could have come from.

4 She remembered that her neighbour, Mr Jones, kept some dangerous snakes in his house.

5 Maybe they had escaped from their tanks.

6 He wasn't moving and his eyes were closed.

7 'I was just having a nap before lunch.'

Useful language Reported speech

3a Look at the examples of direct speech from Erik's story (a–g). Answer the questions below.

a 'I've just had a message from my dad,' she explained to her friend. 'He said there are snakes in the kitchen.'

b 'Are you OK, Dad?' she called.

c 'Yes, absolutely fine,' replied her dad.

d 'I was just having a nap before lunch.'

e 'But what happened to the snakes in the kitchen?' asked Angela.

f 'Snakes!' exclaimed her dad.

g 'I meant snacks! My phone must have changed my spelling!'

1 Which reporting verbs did Erik use?

2 Do we always need to use a reporting verb?

b Look at these examples from Erik's story (a–f). Answer the questions below.

a He said there are snakes in the kitchen.

b He told me to come home immediately.

c She knew she needed to get home as quickly as possible.

d As she was running home, she wondered where the snakes could have come from.

e She remembered that her neighbour, Mr Jones, kept some dangerous snakes in his house.

f Maybe they had escaped from their tanks.

1 Which examples are reported speech? Which are reported thoughts?

2 What did the person actually say/think in each case?

3 Which example is a reported question? Which is a reported instruction?

4 Find three examples of backshifting (= a change in the choice of tense, e.g. from present tense to past tense).

5 Why is there no backshifting in example **a**? What about example **d**?

6 What is unusual about example **f**?

c Change the examples in 3a from direct speech to reported speech.

4 Look at these reporting verbs. Choose one of the reporting verbs to report the direct speech below. Invent any extra details you need.

add	admit	agree	announce	argue	believe
boast	claim	complain	confirm	decide	deny
doubt	enquire	guess	hope	imagine	explain
inform	insist	mention	order	persuade	predict
promise	regret	remark	remind	repeat	reply
report	state	suggest	suppose	warn	wonder

> **Tip!** It's best to include a mixture of direct and reported speech in your story. If you just use one or the other, it can be boring. And don't forget to report people's thoughts too! It can be very powerful in a story.

1 'I'm much better at this game than you.'

Example Robert boasted that he was much better at the game than Helen.

2 'I don't think your plan will work.'

3 'Don't forget to call me when you arrive.'

4 'How about starting again from the beginning?'

5 'How much longer will this journey take?'

6 'I didn't tell anyone your secret.'

7 'There must be over a thousand people here, I'd say.'

Useful language Modals of probability in the past

5a Look at these sentences. In which sentences is the speaker sure of what he or she is saying?

1 'She must have had an accident,' suggested Luke.

2 'The snakes might have escaped,' warned Vicky.

3 'It can't have been David – he's on holiday this week!' insisted Diane.

4 'You may have heard this story before,' explained Thomas.

5 'Could it all have been a misunderstanding?' wondered Annie.

b Underline the past forms of the modal verbs in each sentence.

c Rewrite the underlined sentences using some of the past forms of modal verbs in Exercise 5a.

1 The door was wide open and the parrot was missing. <u>Maybe it had escaped or maybe somebody had stolen it</u>.

2 There were dirty footprints all over the house. <u>It was clear that somebody had broken in</u>.

3 Jacob heard a loud growling sound. <u>Is it possible that it was a lion?</u>

4 <u>'There's no way they've finished yet</u>,' insisted Phil. 'They've only just started.'

6a Read this story that a student called Tanya wrote for the writing task on page 42. Choose a suitable title for the story.

When Angela saw the message on her phone, she ran out of the room. 'You're in the wrong room,' the message said. 'The exam is in room 1742.'

Angela was already stressed about her English exam, which was due to start in six minutes, but now she felt a hundred times worse. Where on earth was room 1742? And who could have sent that message?

Just then, she noticed a small black cat sitting at the foot of a flight of stairs. The cat was staring at her intensely. Suddenly, the cat turned away and ran up the stairs. Angela followed nervously.

At the top of the stairs, Angela saw the cat again. It was at the far end of the corridor. It stood by a large wooden door and then it disappeared. Had it tried to tell her something? She must have imagined it. Nevertheless, Angela hurried along the corridor. She gasped as she saw the sign on the door: 'Room 1742: English exam today.' She was there just in time. And she knew exactly what she would write about for her story.

b Find examples of the following things in Tanya's story.

a an animal

b a mistake

c speech marks

d reported speech or thoughts

e past forms of modal verbs

c Do you prefer Erik's or Tanya's story? Why?

Write your answer in **140–190** words in an appropriate style **on the separate answer sheet**.

Your teacher has asked you to write a story for a class story competition.

Story competition

Your story must **begin** with this sentence:

When Leo saw the box in the shop window, he knew he had to buy it.

Your story must include:
- a friend
- a surprise

The winning story will be published in the school magazine.

Write your **story**.

Tip! Don't forget to include all the information in the question!

Check! Have you:

☐ used direct and reported speech and thoughts?

☐ used descriptive adjectives and adverbs?

☐ added extra information to show how the people felt?

☐ given your story an interesting title?

☐ written between 140 and 190 words?

In Part 1 you:

- **listen**   to eight short recordings, with either one or two people speaking
- **answer**   a multiple-choice question with three options for each recording
- **hear**   each recording twice

1 🎧 1 **Read these examples of multiple-choice questions and extracts from the recording. For each question, choose the correct answer from the three options. Underline the words in the text that give you the answer.**

Tip! Before you listen, read the sentence which introduces the recording. Think about the topic and what you know about it. This will help you to follow for his friend the conversation.

1   You hear two teenagers talking about what to do on their friend's birthday.

Why do they choose to go to the city-centre cinema?

> **Boy:** It's Daisy's birthday soon, isn't it? What are we going to do for her?
>
> **Girl:** Hmm, I don't know, she's hard to please. How about the new multiplex? There's that new film she wanted to see.
>
> **Boy:** Yes, but it's really hard to get there. If we want to invite lots of people, I think it'd be better to go to the cinema in the city centre. What do you think?
>
> **Girl:** I guess so. It's not as nice, but you're right, it's bigger, lots of buses go there and I'm sure loads of people will want to come!

A it has the best choice of films.
B the location is convenient.
C Their friend likes it there.

2   You hear a boy leaving a voicemail message for his friend.

He wants to know what time his friend will …

> Hi Ali, hope you're doing OK. I guess you're busy. I just wanted to drop by your place later to give you the new science books we need. When you get this message can you let me know what time you'll be back from football training? Just text me if I don't answer – I've got a guitar lesson this afternoon so I might not pick up. See you later. Cheers!

A be at football training
B be able to come to his house
C be at home

3   You hear a woman talking about how to prepare for a marathon.

What does she say about eating on the day of the race?

> The first thing to remember is to drink enough water – at least one litre before you start the race and one litre per hour afterwards. You don't want to get dehydrated. Carbohydrates are vital too, so have a good breakfast, with some eggs for protein. Don't go overboard 'cos you'll refuel during the run. You don't have to stretch too much beforehand, but do a light warm-up to get your muscles ready. Some people like to do yoga, but I think you should do whatever gets you ready. The most important thing is to visualise the end of the race, and enjoy it! Good luck!

A Drink less than a litre of water before you start.
B Eat as much as you can on the morning of the race.
C Don't have too much for breakfast because you'll eat again later.

4 You hear two friends talking about going fishing.

What does the boy offer to do for the girl?

> **Boy:** Have you ever tried fishing?
>
> **Girl:** No, but I'm up for it. What do I need to get started?
>
> **Boy:** Well, the first thing is a good rod and some sharp hooks. It's a good idea to bring a little stool too, 'cos you'll be sitting for a while.
>
> **Girl:** Hmm, OK. Do I need to buy all of that?
>
> **Boy:** No, I've got some spares you can borrow. You'll need to buy a special fishing licence too. You can pick that up on the way.
>
> **Girl:** OK. What else?
>
> **Boy:** Lots of patience! It's great for relaxation, though.
>
> **Girl:** Sounds good.

A lend her some equipment

B get her a licence

C teach her how to do it

5 You hear a boy talking to a shop assistant.

What does he have a problem with?

> **Shop assistant:** Hi there, can I help you?
>
> **Boy:** Yeah, I was in here last week and picked this up, but it's stopped working.
>
> **Shop assistant:** OK, let me take a look. OK. Let's see … um… Let me just try and see if it is working. I'll plug it in over here. It seems to be working fine. Did you try another socket?
>
> **Boy:** Yes, but it still wouldn't work with my phone.
>
> **Shop assistant:** Can I see your phone?
>
> **Boy:** Sure, here you go.
>
> **Shop assistant:** I see the port is a bit blocked. I'll just clean it up … There you go!
>
> **Boy:** That's great, thanks!

A a phone

B a charger

C a phone case

2 Look at the options below. Two teenagers are discussing a television programme they have both watched. Which of the phrases are used to agree with the other speaker? Which are used to disagree? Write A or D.

a Hmm, I don't know … ....

b 100%. ....

c Yes, but … ....

d Don't you think that … ....

e But if … ....

f Exactly. ....

g OK, yes. ....

h Yes, of course! ....

> **Tip!** It is often easier to hear when people are agreeing than when they are disagreeing. While listening, try to identify the specific items people are agreeing and disagreeing about.

3 🎧 2 Now listen to the recording and answer the question below.

You hear two students discussing a television programme they both watched.

What do they disagree about?

A how difficult the living conditions shown in the programme were.

B how the people shown in the programme must have felt about their living conditions.

C how much living conditions have changed since the time shown in the programme.

🎧 3 You will hear people talking in eight different situations. For questions **1–8**, choose the best answer (**A**, **B** or **C**).

---

1   You hear two students talking about their first geography class of the year.
    How do they both feel?

    A   optimistic about how the classes will develop over the term
    B   concerned that it was more difficult than they'd expected
    C   satisfied that they'd learnt some valuable information

2   You hear a boy telling a friend about buying some food for wild birds.
    What is he aiming to do?

    A   attract one particular species of bird
    B   keep the local birds alive during the winter
    C   monitor the range of wild birds that visit his garden

3   You hear a girl telling a friend about a spelling competition she won.
    What does she say about it?

    A   She took some time to find a strategy that worked for her.
    B   She found that her good visual memory helped her the most.
    C   She wasn't concerned by the level of the other competitors.

4   You hear a technology teacher telling her students about the model cars they are going to make.
    What does she warn them about?

    A   being inaccurate as they develop their model
    B   choosing a car that's too complicated for them to make
    C   finding they need tools that the school doesn't currently have

5   You hear a boy talking to his sister about a sweatshirt he bought recently.
    Why is he unhappy with it?

    A   He's worried it may already have gone out of fashion.
    B   He feels it's poor quality for the price he paid.
    C   He thinks the colour doesn't suit him at all.

6   You hear a school football coach talking to his team about avoiding injuries.
    What does he propose for this season?

    A   checking players drink enough fluids before training and matches
    B   improving the exercises at the start of their training sessions.
    C   making a specific type of training a regular event

7   You hear a girl talking to her friend about a building she's just visited.
    Why is she telling her about it?

    A   to recommend it as somewhere worth visiting
    B   to confirm that her opinion about it was correct
    C   to explain why she decided to go there

8   You hear a boy leaving a phone message for a friend about a family camping holiday.
    What does he say about the holiday?

    A   They feel inspired to repeat the experience.
    B   They managed to make the best of a bad situation.
    C   They were disappointed after all their preparation.

Tip! Remember that you can listen twice to each recording. Use the second listening to confirm your answer. If you're still not sure, then have a guess – don't leave any questions unanswered.

Advice

*1 Remember you are looking for something that **both** speakers feel. What do they say about the class? Has each of them learnt something from it? Was it useful?*

5 What item of clothing are the speakers talking about? Why did the boy want to return it to the shop? What does he mean by 'charge'?

In Part 2 you:

- **listen** to a recording with one speaker
- **write down** words from the recording to complete the sentences
- **hear** the answers in the same order as the recording

1a Read exam question 9 below. What words might fit in the gap, which could describe a house?

You will hear a girl talking about vacations in her country.

She says that the house is **(9)** ....

> **Tip!** You know the context, so try to guess what type of information could fit each gap. This will help you to hear the correct answer when you listen to the recording.

b Read the extract from the audioscript below. Which is the answer to question 9? Underline the part of the audioscript that contains the correct answer. Which other adjectives appear in the script? What do they describe?

> The most important part is that all the family's together. So people take time off work and travel to all parts of the country, depending on where their relatives are. All the adults have time off work and we're on school holidays as well so there's a real holiday atmosphere! We usually go to my uncle's house on the north coast, which is a beautiful and traditional part of the country. I love going there to his place 'cos it's absolutely massive.

c 🎧 4 Listen to the recording and check your answer.

2a Look at question 10. What possibilities could fit in the gap?

The girl says that her **(10)** .... do something which she finds surprising during the holiday.

> **Tip!** Identify what kind of word goes in the gap. Is it singular or plural? Looking at the words immediately before and after the gap can help you to do this.

b 🎧 5 Listen to the recording. How many different family members are mentioned? What do we learn about them?

> Everyone stays over and me and my brothers love seeing our cousins. We have a big family so there's always loads of people there. Everyone sleeps on sofas in the living room – even my parents don't sleep in a bedroom! The day after we get there, we have a huge breakfast with fresh juice, eggs, and special cakes and pastries my grandma makes, before we head for the beach. I always look forward to that!

3a Read the sentences and think of ONE word which fits each gap.

1 Of all the people in my family, my .... are the funniest.

2 When we're on holiday, there's so much .... in the house!

3 On the beach it gets really hot, so you have to be .... of the sun.

3b Choose the correct option to complete the information about the sentences in Exercise 3a.

1 In sentence 1, the word in the gap is followed by a *plural / singular* verb form, which means that it must be a *plural / singular* noun.

2 In sentence 2 the word in the gap comes after *so much*, which means that it must be *a countable / an uncountable* noun.

3 In sentence 3, the word in the gap follows 'be' and in this context it must be an *adjective / adverb*.

🎧 6 You will hear a girl called Anna giving a presentation about the fashion blog that she's created. For questions **9–18**, complete the sentences with a word or short phrase.

Tip! Use the time before the recording starts to read the rubric and find out who will be talking and the topic. Read quickly through the sentences. What type of information are you listening for?

Anna – fashion blogger

After Anna was featured in a **(9)** .... , she had more people visiting her blog.

Anna now has a **(10)** .... to help her develop the blog.

When choosing clothes for her blog, the **(11)** .... of Anna's readers is the most important point she considers.

Anna thinks teenagers are likely to spend more on **(12)** .... than on other items of clothing.

Anna prefers buying her own clothes from **(13)** .... rather than other places.

The historical period that's given Anna the greatest inspiration for her blog is the **(14)** ....

Clothes with **(15)** .... on them recently attracted attention to Anna's blog.

Anna mainly promotes clothes made of materials such as **(16)** .... on her blog.

Among the things Anna has made herself, people have showed most interest in her **(17)** ....

Anna was pleased that visitors to the blog have described it as being **(18)** ....

Advice

12 Can you predict an answer here? Read the whole sentence. What **type** of word will the answer be?

16 Anna is going to give an **example** of materials. Think of some names of common materials used to make clothes. Listen carefully – which is the answer and which are the distractors?

In Part 3 you:

- **hear**   five different people talking about related things
- **match**   what they say with one of eight options

1a Imagine a new fast-food restaurant has opened in your town. How might you feel about it? Here are some examples:

> A   pleased with the value for money
>
> B   impressed with the service
>
> C   disappointed with the food
>
> D   shocked at the price
>
> E   surprised by the choice of location

Tip! The options for Part 3 might include feelings or opinions, which have to be matched to with what the speakers say in the recordings.

b How would you express these feelings? Think about the words and phrases you might use.

2a 🎧 7 Now read what Speakers 1–5 are saying about a fast–food restaurant in their town. Which of the options A–E matches what each speaker says? Underline parts of the audioscript that give you the answers, then listen.

> **1** I honestly think it's exactly what our town needs. What struck me was there's a real demand for reasonably priced food like this. It's the 21st century and we want the same things that you can find in other towns. Tourists who come to our area will definitely go to this place, too, so it'll have a knock-on effect to the local economy. I honestly can't see anything wrong with it. I've already been there a couple of times and can't wait to go again!

> **2** Well I don't have a real problem with it, but I just don't see why it's been opened here. We've got loads of options already. What we really need is more places to spend our free time, more activities, that sort of thing. But if people want to spend their money there, then that's up to them.

> **3** I'm not really bothered to be honest with you. I don't go in for fancy eating and posh service anyway. Give me a sandwich and I'll be happy. And have you seen what they charge there? What a rip-off!

> **4** Well I went there and I was really put off. I had high hopes but I just wasn't that impressed. The burgers weren't up to much and even the chips were cold! It was OK, but certainly not worth all the hype. I won't be rushing back.

> **5** The food was great, the staff were really friendly and I loved it. Honestly, I just think that people around here need to stop complaining and try something different. Yes, it's more expensive than other places, but you have to pay for quality, don't you? I think it's great and hope that other places of the same quality open up here soon as well.

b Compare your answers with a partner. How did you know which option was the correct match for each speaker?

🎧 8 You will hear five short extracts in which teenagers are talking about finding a valuable object by chance. For questions **19–23**, choose from the list (**A–H**) what each speaker says about the experience.
Use the letters only once. There are three extra letters which you do not need to use.

Tip! Remember that you will hear five different speakers, but you have eight options to choose from. Read carefully through the options before you start listening, so that you know what information you're listening for when the recording starts.

A   It led to a new interest for me.

B   I managed to return it to its owner.   Speaker 1 [ ] 19

C   I made a disappointing discovery about it.
                                                          Speaker 2 [ ] 20

D   I helped to prevent it from getting lost again.
                                                          Speaker 3 [ ] 21

E   I was tempted to keep it.
                                                          Speaker 4 [ ] 22

F   It helped me to achieve what I'd always wanted.

G   It led to a new idea for an invention.   Speaker 5 [ ] 23

H   I was given a cash reward.

Advice

21 The speaker mentions an *idea*. Whose idea was it? What was it for?

23 The speaker mentions a collection. What has she started to collect? Why?

In Part 4 you:

- **listen**   to a recording of two people speaking
- **answer**   seven multiple-choice questions, each with three options

1   Work with a partner. Discuss the questions below.

1   Have you ever volunteered for something?   **2**   What kind of voluntary work might people choose to do?

2   🎧 9 **Listen to an interview with a girl called Sophia, who's talking about a volunteer project at her school. Then answer this question:**

How did the students initially feel about volunteering?

A They were nervous about it.

B They had lots of ideas of how to start.

C They didn't think they had any relevant skills.

3a   🎧 10 **Now cover options A–C and the extract from the audioscript below, and just read the question. Listen to the next part of the interview and write down the answer as you listen.**

So what did the students get out of the project?

b   **Now look at the three options below. Which one matches your answer the most closely? Compare your answers with a partner. Then look at the audioscript and underline the part that gives you the answer.**

A They practised new skills.

B They learnt how to use social media.

C They taught other people how to use social media.

> **Interviewer:** So what did the students get out of the project?
> **Sophia:** There were two charities and one community association that took us up on that offer. Basically they loved it because it was a way for them to connect with a new audience, which would've been very difficult and time-consuming for them to set up themselves. But it was also a way of using our skills. It allowed my classmates running the accounts to be creative in using social media. It forced them to leave their comfort zone and try something different.

4   🎧 11 **Now listen to the final part of Sophia's interview. Read the question below and choose the correct option, A, B or C.**

> **Interviewer:** That's amazing. And what about the future of this project?
> **Sophia:** Well, I am worried about it. We're all finishing school this year and most of us are going off to university in the city, so we won't be in the local area any more. However, we're talking to a number of charities and organisations to see if we can find a way to continue doing what we've started. It would be a real shame if everything just stopped when we leave school. Hopefully we'll find a way to do this, and carry on with what we started.
> **Interviewer:** Thanks for talking to us today, Sophia – we look forward to hearing more about the project.

What is Sophia worried about?

A Going to university

B Leaving the local area

C The possibility of the project ending

🎧12 You will hear an interview with a student called John Benton, who's just completed a 25-kilometre running race. For questions **24–30**, choose the best answer (**A**, **B** or **C**).

Tip! The questions follow the order of the recording. The interviewer's questions will signal when you need to move to the next question.

24 Why did John decide to enter the race?

   A   He was encouraged by his father to take part.
   B   He wanted to prove his friends wrong.
   C   He was inspired by a celebrity's achievements.

25 One feature of John's training before the event was to

   A   get some rest between training sessions.
   B   leave himself enough time to build up his fitness.
   C   set targets that he felt were realistic.

26 John says that once he started training, he had difficulties

   A   fitting it in around his usual school schedule.
   B   finding time for leisure activities after school.
   C   making himself run in cold weather before school.

27 What does John say about his diet before the race?

   A   decided not to follow a very strict diet.
   B   left it almost too late to adopt a suitable diet.
   C   was unwilling to give up his favourite foods.

28 What particularly encouraged John on the day of the race?

   A   The atmosphere was much more positive than he'd expected.
   B   People he'd never met before were wishing him well.
   C   Some people in the crowd were there to support him personally.

29 One strategy John used to keep himself going was to

   A   maintain a fairly even running speed throughout the race.
   B   ignore any negative thoughts about failure.
   C   keep in mind the finishing time he wanted to achieve.

30 Immediately after John finished the race, he

   A   was almost too tired to notice people congratulating him.
   B   promised himself he would never attempt another one.
   C   celebrated his achievements with friends.

Advice

24 Whose attitude *made John want to compete?*

25 *Listen for another word that means the same as* **targets***.*

In Part 1 you:

- **talk** to the examiner, not your partner
- **answer** questions about yourself and your life, e.g. your name, free-time activities, family, future plans

Tip! There are always two examiners in the exam room. One will conduct the Speaking test with you. The other will only listen and make notes. Don't panic when you see the second examiner writing notes – it doesn't mean you're making lots of mistakes!

Focus Before you begin

1 Read the advice for the Speaking test. Match each piece of advice with a reason.

1 Wear smart but comfortable clothes.
2 Come to the exam centre in good time for the exam.
3 If you feel yourself getting stressed, breathe deeply and slowly.
4 Make friends with your partner.
5 Speak with your partner in English while you're waiting.

a The examiner will not mind you taking a moment to calm down.
b It'll make it easier to talk to him/her during the exam.
c This will get you into 'English-speaking mode' – ready for the test.
d It's good to make a good impression, but you also need to feel relaxed.
e It's better to wait half an hour than to get stressed about being late or lost.

Focus Understanding the task

2a Read the information about Part 1 of the Speaking test.

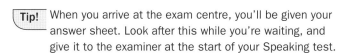

Tip! When you arrive at the exam centre, you'll be given your answer sheet. Look after this while you're waiting, and give it to the examiner at the start of your Speaking test.

- You'll take the Speaking test in pairs. If there's an odd number of candidates, there will be one group of three. The total time for the Speaking test is 14 minutes (20 minutes for a group of three). The time for the test is fixed, so the examiners may have to stop you in the middle of an answer.

- Part 1 takes about 2 minutes (3 minutes for a group of three).

- At the start of the test, the examiner will welcome you and ask for your answer sheet. The examiner will introduce himself/herself and his/her colleague and ask your name and where you're from.

- The examiner will ask you and your partner questions about yourselves for two minutes.

- Part 1 is your chance to make a good first impression. Avoid one-word answers, but also don't expect to give long, detailed answers. There's only two minutes for your questions and answers, plus your partner's questions and answers. A good answer is usually about two sentences long.

- The examiner may smile and nod his/her head, but he/she won't comment on your answers. The examiner can't help you if you get stuck, but can repeat the question if necessary.

b Look at these statements about Part 1 of the Speaking test. Are the statements true or false?

1 You can take the Speaking test in pairs or threes.
2 If the examiner tells you to stop talking, it's because he/she thinks your answer is boring.
3 You should give extremely detailed answers to every question.
4 When you are speaking, the examiner might say things like 'Really? That's interesting.'
5 The examiner is allowed to repeat questions.

Useful language Interview

3a Where are you from? Read three good answers to this question. Underline words and phrases you could use in your own answer.

1 I'm from Puerto Varas, which is about a thousand kilometres south of here. It's in the mountains, and it's really popular with tourists.

2 I live right in the heart of the city, not far from the university. It's really handy for my studies but it can get quite noisy at times.

3 Well, I grew up in the middle of nowhere, in a small village in the Lake District. But now I live on the outskirts of the capital.

b How would you answer the question?

4a What do you do in your free time? Complete these good answers with prepositions from the box.

by	for	into	of	on

1 I'm really keen .... painting, so I tend to spend most of my free time doing that.

2 I don't really have time .... hobbies because I have three younger brothers and sisters and I'm always really busy looking after them.

3 I've been .... football since I was a child. I play regularly, and I also love watching live matches.

4 I'm a big fan .... jazz, so I spend a lot of time listening to jazz CDs and trying to develop my skills as a pianist.

5 When I'm not studying, I relax .... reading books or playing computer games, for example.

b How would you answer the question?

> **Tip!** Link your ideas together with words like 'because' and 'so'.

Test 1 Exam practice Speaking • Part 1 (interview)

1 Work with a partner. Take turns to ask and answer these questions. Ask questions in any order.

> **Tip!** Look at the tenses / verb forms in the questions. Your answer will usually start with the same tense or verb form as in the question. For example: *Would you like to …? Yes, I would. Has the kind of music you like changed …? No, it hasn't. I still like to …*

Part 1   2 minutes [3 minutes for groups of three]

Interlocutor	First we'd like to know something about you.
	Music
	• What kind of music do you listen to in your free time? (Why?)
	• Has the kind of music you like changed in the last few years? (Why? / Why not?)
	• Do you listen to the same kind of music as your friends?
	• Would you like to be able to play a musical instrument? (Why? / Why not?)
	• Have you ever been to a live concert? (Why? / Why not)

2 🎧13 Now listen to the recording and answer the questions you hear.

In Part 2 you:

- **talk** about two photos by yourself
- **compare** your photos and answer a question about them
- **listen** while your partner is talking about his/her photos
- **answer** one short question about your partner's photos

Focus Understanding the task

1a Read about Part 2 of the Speaking test.

- Part 2 takes about 4 minutes (6 minutes for a group of three).
- The examiner will give you a sheet of paper with two photos on it. A question is printed at the top of the page.
- He/She will ask you to compare the two photos and answer the question. You have a minute to speak about the photos by yourself.
- You aren't given any time to plan your answer, so you should start speaking straight away, giving your first impressions of the photos.
- At the end, the examiner will ask your partner a question about your photos.
- The examiner will give your partner some photos too. While your partner is describing his/her own photos, listen carefully and be ready to answer a short follow-up question about them.

b Are these statements true or false?

1 You and your partner both talk for a minute about the same photos.

2 You need to describe everything you can see in the photos.

3 If you can't remember the question, you need to ask the examiner to repeat it.

4 The examiner will allow you to keep talking until you have answered the question.

5 You should spend about 20–30 seconds answering the follow-up question.

> **Tip!** Don't spend too much time describing the people and objects you can see in the photos. Focus more on the stories behind the photos, e.g. how the people are feeling, what is happening.

2a 🎧14 Look at photos A and B on page C1. Listen to the examiner's instructions and two candidates, Kevin and Salwa, discussing the photos.

b Discuss in pairs.

1 Why did the examiner stop Kevin in the middle of his answer?

2 Do you think he will lose marks because of this?

3 What was the follow-up question?

Focus Comparing photos

Tip! Make sure you use linking words and phrases. The examiner will be listening for the way you connect your ideas together.

3a Match the techniques with the examples from Kevin's answer.

1 Use *both* to show what the two photos have in common.

2 Use words like *while* or *whereas* to show a contrast between two things in the same sentence.

3 Use phrases like *on the other hand* or *in contrast* to show a contrast between two longer sentences.

4 Use phrases like *One key difference is …* and *The biggest difference is …* to introduce key contrasts.

5 Use comparative adjectives or adverbs.

a The first one looks like … The second picture, in contrast, shows …

b The second photo shows a much busier scene.

c Probably the biggest difference, though, is where the light is coming from.

d In the first picture, there's just the sun, the moon and … one star, while in the second picture, it's all artificial light.

e They both show beautiful night-time scenes.

b Look at the photos on page C2. Make notes of the similarities and differences between them.

c Use the techniques from Exercise 3a to make sentences to compare the photos.

Tip! It's usually easier to compare the photos first (for 30–40 seconds) and then answer the question (for 20–30 seconds). But if you answer the question while you're comparing, that's fine too.

Useful language Answering the questions

4a Which of these questions did Kevin answer for the long turn? Which was the follow-up question for Salwa?

- Which of these situations would you prefer to be in?
- Why are the people outside at night?

b Here are some useful phrases for answering Part 2 questions. Decide whether they would be more useful for answering Kevin's long-turn question or for answering Salwa's short follow-up question. Write *Long* or *Short* next to each phrase.

1 As for why the people… ....

2 I definitely prefer the first situation because … ....

3 I can imagine they're … ....

4 It appears to be some kind of … ....

5 As my partner said, … ....

6 They seem to be waiting … ....

7 It looks as if they've probably … ....

8 I'd much rather be in the second situation … ....

9 As far as I can tell, they're … ....

10 My partner mentioned …, and yes, I'd certainly agree that … ....

11 The people might be on their way to … ....

12 The second situation looks a lot more appealing to me because … ....

13 I think I'd choose the second situation because … ....

Tip! The long-turn question is usually about the people in the photos, e.g. you might be asked why the people have chosen to do something, or what they are enjoying about it. The follow-up question is usually about you, e.g. you might be asked which of the two situations you prefer and why.

5 Work with a partner. Take turns to answer this question about the pictures on page C2.

Which of the two situations would you prefer to be in? Why?

Tip! For the follow-up question, don't think too hard about which situation you'd prefer. Just make a quick decision and justify it.

Look at the exam instructions below and photos on pages C3 and C4. Then do this exam task in pairs.

| Part 2 | 4 minutes [6 minutes for groups of three] |

Interlocutor In this part of the test, I'm going to give each of you two photographs. I'd like you to talk about your photographs on your own for about a minute, and also to answer a question about your partner's photographs.

(*Candidate A*), it's your turn first. Here are your photographs on page C3 of the Speaking appendix. They show **friends on a day out**.

I'd like you to compare the photographs, and say **what you think the friends are enjoying about their day out**.

All right?

Candidate A

🕐 *1 minute* ....

Interlocutor Thank you.

(*Candidate B*), **which of these things would you prefer to do with friends? (Why?)**

Candidate B

🕐 *Approximately 30 seconds* ....

Interlocutor Thank you.

Now (*Candidate B*), here are your photographs on page C4 of the Speaking appendix. They show **people doing exercise in different ways**.

I'd like you to compare the photographs, and say **why you think the people have decided to do exercise in these ways**.

All right?

Candidate B

🕐 *1 minute* ....

Interlocutor Thank you.

(*Candidate A*), **which of these exercises would you prefer to do? (Why?)**

Candidate A

🕐 *Approximately 30 seconds* ....

Interlocutor Thank you.

In Part 3 you:

- **talk** with a partner
- **discuss** some written ideas
- **try** to reach a decision together with your partner

Focus Understanding the task

1a Read about Part 3 of the Speaking test.

> **Tip!** It's good to start with a summary of the situation and the five ideas.

- Part 3 takes about 4 minutes (5 minutes for a group of three).
- The examiner will show you and your partner a page with a discussion question and five ideas to help in your discussion.
- You have fifteen seconds to read the information and start thinking.
- You then spend 2 minutes (3 minutes for a group of three) discussing the question and ideas together with your partner. You don't need to discuss all the ideas.
- The examiner will then ask a follow-up question where you need to choose the best ideas from the ones on the page.
- You have 1 minute to try to reach a decision.
- There is no correct answer, and you won't lose marks if you fail to reach a decision. But you must show that you're trying to work together.

b Are these statements true or false?

1 This part of the test focuses on your ability to communicate well with other people in English.

2 You need to start speaking as soon as you see the question.

3 You need to discuss all five ideas on the page.

4 Groups of three can spend longer on the follow-up question.

5 You will lose marks if you don't reach a decision in time.

2a Look at the Part 3 task on page C5. Try to think of one or two points you could make about each of the five ideas.

b 🎧15 Listen to Kevin and Salwa discussing the question. Which of your ideas did they mention?

Focus Inviting your partner to speak

3a When you invite your partner to speak, you demonstrate that you can work collaboratively. Complete these extracts from Kevin and Salwa's discussion.

> **Tip!** Always respond to your partner's ideas and answer his/her questions. This shows that you are listening to your partner and considering his/her ideas.

1 What .... think, Salwa?

2 Really? What makes .... that?

3 What .... mean?

4 OK, so .... education?

5 Our school system expects us to learn foreign languages .... ?

b 🎧15 Question tags allow you to express your opinion and then invite your partner to speak. Complete these question tags from Kevin and Salwa's discussion. Then listen again to check.

1 … it makes foreign travel much easier if you speak the local language, ___doesn't it___ ?

2 That'd just be impossible, ... ?

3 … translation software is getting better all the time, ... ?

4 Most of us don't have friends or family who speak a different language, ... ?

5 You'll certainly need to understand the local language if you want to do that, ... ?

6 I suppose we can forget about technology straight away, ... ?

7 We talked about travel, ... , so let's say that's one of our main reasons, ... ?

Focus Disagreeing politely

4a You don't need to agree with everything your partner says, but if you disagree, you need to be polite. Look at these extracts from Kevin and Salwa's discussion. Choose the best way of disagreeing politely.

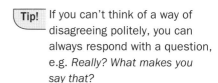

Tip! If you can't think of a way of disagreeing politely, you can always respond with a question, e.g. *Really? What makes you say that?*

1 Well, obviously it makes foreign travel much easier if you speak the local language, doesn't it?

   a That's true, but we can't expect to learn the language of every country we visit.

   b Not really. We can't expect to learn the language of every country we visit, can we?

2 In my experience, all you really need is English. What do you think?

   a Well, no, there are lots of places where English won't help.

   b Well, it depends where you want to go.

3 So it'll still be worth learning languages so we can have proper conversations.

   a Hmmm, maybe you're right. But I'd say that affects only a small percentage of people.

   b Are you serious? Surely that affects only a small percentage of people.

4 Well, the obvious answer is: yes, because our school system expects us to learn foreign languages, doesn't it?

   a I disagree. That's not a reason for learning something.

   b Yes. But that's not really a good reason for learning something.

5 You'll certainly need to understand the local language if you want to study abroad, won't you?

   a Well, I understand what you're saying, but I'm not sure it's worth studying several languages at school.

   b Possibly, but surely it's not worth studying several languages at school.

b Work in pairs. Do you agree or disagree with these statements? Say if you agree and add your own point. If you disagree, try to do it politely.

1 If you want a good job, you really need to speak another language fluently.

2 I think the best reason for learning a language is that it's so much fun.

3 I don't think I'd want to learn a language just to make friends.

c Work with a partner. Discuss the question on page C6. Respond to your partner's comments by agreeing or disagreeing politely.

Look at the exam instructions below and the question and ideas on page C7, then do this task in pairs.

Tip! Listen carefully for the decision you need to make, because this is not written down. If you don't hear it properly, or if you forget, you can ask the examiner to repeat it.

Part 3   4 minutes [5 minutes for groups of three]

Interlocutor Now I'd like you to talk about something together for about two minutes.

Some people think it's necessary to keep up to date with the latest world news, and other people disagree. Here are some reasons why it might or might not be useful to keep up to date and a question for you to discuss.

First you have some time to look at the task on page C7 of the Speaking appendix.

Now talk to each other about **whether it's necessary for everyone to keep up to date with world news.**

Candidates

🕐 *2 minutes (3 minutes for groups of three)*

Interlocutor Thank you. Now you have about a minute to decide **which is the most important reason for keeping up to date with world news.**

Candidates

🕐 *1 minute (for pairs and groups of three)*

Interlocutor Thank you.

In Part 4 you:

- **speak** with the examiner and the other candidate(s)
- **answer** questions that are related to the topic in Part 3

Focus Understanding the task

1a Read the information about Part 4 of the Speaking test.

- Part 4 takes about 4 minutes (6 minutes for a group of three).
- The examiner will ask a series of questions related to the topic in Part 3.
- The examiner will ask some questions to you, some to your partner(s), and some for you to discuss together.
- After your partner has finished speaking, the examiner may ask your opinion on the same question.
- This section is similar to Part 1: both parts involve questions and answers without any visual prompts. However, the questions in Part 1 ask mainly for information; the questions in Part 4 ask mainly for evaluation.

b Are these statements true or false?

1 Part 4 is longer for groups of three.

2 There will be one question for you and one for your partner.

3 The questions mainly ask you for personal information.

2a Look at some examples of Part 4 questions. These are on the same topic as Kevin and Salwa's discussion from Part 3. Which questions would you find easier to answer?

1 Would you like to be able to speak lots of languages?

2 Do you think some people are naturally better at languages than others?

3 Some people say they feel like a different person when they're speaking a different language. What do you think?

4 How long does it take to learn a foreign language?

5 If you decided to study in a country where the first language is different from your own, what challenges might you face?

6 Some people say the best way to learn a language is to make friends with people who speak that language. What do you think?

b 🎧16 Listen to Kevin and Salwa discussing some of these questions. Which question do they answer together? Which one do they answer separately? Which question does only one person answer?

c How did Salwa help Kevin during Part 4?

> **Tip!** Part 4 is the examiner's chance to make a final decision. If one candidate has spoken a lot more than the other for Parts 1–3, the examiner may use Part 4 to focus attention on the quieter candidate. So don't worry if you aren't asked the same number of questions.

> **Tip!** You can use phrases like *I'm not really sure, I've never really thought about it like that* and *Wow ... that's a difficult question* to give yourself time to think. But if you use one of these phrases, you still need to answer the question afterwards!

Useful language Conditionals

3a 🎧16 Match the beginnings and endings of these extracts from Kevin and Salwa's conversation. Then listen to the conversation again to check.

1 If you just want to survive in a different country, and you're living there,

2 I think if you studied hard during that time,

3 If you only have a few lessons each week,

4 I feel a lot more comfortable

5 But if they knew how hard I've had to work to get to this level,

6 It's just hard work, and anybody can do it

a if I'm climbing an indoor climbing wall, rather than a rock face I've never seen before.

b they wouldn't be so jealous!

c you'd be able to buy the basics, like food and clothes.

d if they're prepared to work hard.

e then I guess you could make a lot of progress in just a month.

f it might take five years or more before you start to feel confident.

b Second conditionals are especially useful for answering questions where you don't have much to say. Complete these extracts from Part 4 discussions by putting the verbs in the correct form.

1 Which language would you like to learn?

Well, I don't really want to learn another language, but if I .... **(have)** to choose one, I think it .... **(be)** Japanese.

2 What is the best way of keeping fit?

Well, I've hurt my knee, which means I can't do very much physical exercise. It's quite frustrating. But if I .... **(not / have)** this injury, ... **(I / love)** to go cycling.

3 What kind of films do you enjoy watching?

I don't actually watch many films – I don't have time! But if there .... **(be)** a really good action movie on at the cinema, ... **(I / probably / go)** to see it.

Test 1 Exam practice Speaking • Part 4 (discussion)

Work in groups of three. Ask and answer these questions.

Tip! The examiner can ask simple follow-up questions like *Why?* or *What do you think?* However, don't expect the examiner to join in the discussion or comment on your answers.

| Part 4 | 4 minutes [6 minutes for groups of three] |

Interlocutor

- Should schools encourage students to find out about the news? (Why? / Why not?)

- Do you think 24-hour news channels on television are useful? (Why? / Why not?)

- In your opinion, are people more interested in good news or bad news? (Why?)

- Some people say there is too much information available in today's world. Do you agree? (Why? / Why not?)

- Do you believe everything you read on the internet? (Why? / Why not?)

- Do you think people are too interested in finding out about the lives of celebrities? (Why? / Why not?)

Thank you. That is the end of the test.

> What do you think?
> Do you agree?
> And you?

- How many questions are in this part of the test?
- How many options do you have to choose from in each question?

Useful language Collocations

1 **Choose the correct words or phrases that are used together with the underlined phrases.**

> **Tip!** Organise your vocabulary records in sets like these as it will help you to remember them.

Education and exams

1 I can't believe I got *first / top* <u>marks</u> in the physics exam!

2 It is important that you never *lose / skip* <u>lessons</u> if you want to do well in this subject.

3 Give yourself plenty of time to *review / revise* <u>for the exam</u>. Don't leave it until the night before.

4 The thing I hate the most about school is all the <u>exams</u> we have to *do / make*.

Money

5 Education costs an *awful / awesome* <u>lot of money</u>, but it is definitely worth it.

6 The school *raised / lifted* over £1,000 <u>in donations</u> for the local hospital.

7 My grandad *made / did* <u>a small fortune</u> investing in computer technology in the early days.

8 I always shop online because I get better *value / worth* <u>for money</u>.

Crime

9 Police have *made / done* five <u>arrests</u> in connection with the football riot over the weekend.

10 The defendant was *found / discovered* <u>guilty</u> of burglary and sentenced to two years in prison.

11 Did you see on the news that somebody *robbed / stole* the <u>bank</u> that we use?

12 I've never *committed / done* <u>a crime</u> in my life.

Computer technology

13 *Shift / Click* <u>on the link</u> for more information.

14 *Compress / Combine* <u>the file</u> before you send it by email if it is very large.

15 You will need to *restart / begin* <u>the program</u> after you have updated it.

16 I've *put away / saved* <u>the updated files</u> on a memory stick.

Useful language Confusing words

2 **Match the words with their definitions.**

> steal   rob

1 The focus of this verb is on the person or place that was the victim.

2 The focus of this verb is on the thing that was taken, for example, money.

> borrow   lend

3 This verb means to take something, but with the promise of returning it later.

4 This verb means to give something, but with the expectation that it will be returned later.

advise   advice

5 a noun

6 a verb

affect   effect

7 a noun

8 a verb

already   yet

9 An adverb used to talk about something that happened before now or before a particular time. Usually used in positive statements e.g. I've .... seen that film.

10 An adverb used to talk about something that is expected to happen. Usually used in negative statements or questions e.g. Haven't you seen that film .... ?

take   bring

11 This verb suggests movement towards the speaker.

12 This verb suggests movement away from the speaker.

funny   fun

13 This is used to describe something that is enjoyable.

14 This is used to describe something that makes you laugh.

sympathetic   kind

15 This describes a person who cares about somebody and understands their problems.

16 This describes a person who tries to help people and make them happy.

remind   remember

17 This verb is the opposite of 'forget'.

18 This verb can be used to talk about something that makes you think of an event in the past.

3 **Complete the sentences with a suitable word from Exercise 2.**

1 Whenever I hear this song it .... me of that great holiday we had two years ago.

2 I'm so glad you could join us for this session. Did you .... anything to show us?

3 I'd like your .... on this question in my homework.

4 The principal was very .... to my problem, but he said there was nothing he could do.

5 I was .... while walking home after college. They took my wallet and my phone.

6 I don't believe you've .... done your homework. It only took you 20 minutes!

For questions **1–8**, read the text below and decide which answer (**A**, **B**, **C** or **D**) best fits each gap. There is an example at the beginning (**0**).

Mark your answers **on the separate answer sheet**.

Tip! If you don't know the answer to a question, look carefully at the options and cross out the ones that you know are wrong, then make a guess. Never leave an answer blank – you may guess correctly!

Example:

0   **A**   vast   **B**   wide   **C**   far   **D**   high

0	A	B	C	D
	▬	▭	▭	▭

Why you should read fiction

At school, the **(0)** .... majority of what we learn is factual. In history lessons we memorise names and dates; in science we have to cope **(1)** .... chemical formulas and complex equations; in maths it's all numbers and signs. It's only in language lessons where we may **(2)** .... fiction. Some people would argue that there's **(3)** .... point in reading something which is 'made up'. If this is the **(4)** .... , why do language teachers encourage their students to look at anything **(5)** .... from dictionaries and reference materials?

It is because they are **(6)** .... of the benefits that reading brings. It isn't simply because reading fiction helps us **(7)** .... reality for a while and switch off from our everyday routines. Reading fiction also teaches us to see the world through other people's eyes. It **(8)** .... us to understand the feelings of others, making us more empathetic. Fiction, in other words, helps us be better friends.

1   **A**   for   **B**   on   **C**   by   **D**   with

2   **A**   come up   **B**   come across   **C**   come about   **D**   come over

3   **A**   little   **B**   slight   **C**   minimal   **D**   hardly

4   **A**   issue   **B**   matter   **C**   case   **D**   point

5   **A**   except   **B**   apart   **C**   other   **D**   beside

6   **A**   aware   **B**   wise   **C**   familiar   **D**   sensitive

7   **A**   depart   **B**   miss   **C**   escape   **D**   break

8   **A**   lets   **B**   authorises   **C**   makes   **D**   enables

- Are you given words to choose from in Part 2 questions?
- Why is it important to read the text very carefully before you start to answer the questions?

Useful language Linking expressions

1 Which linking words or conjunctions describe a contrast, a purpose or a time relationship? Write C, P or T next to each item. One of these items can be used in two ways.

1 although	....	**7** in spite of	....
2 as soon as	....	**8** meanwhile	....
3 despite	....	**9** so that	....
4 even though	....	**10** whereas	....
5 however	....	**11** while	....
6 in order to	....		

2 The underlined linking expressions from Exercise 1 have all been used incorrectly. Write the correct linking expressions on the lines.

> **Tip!** Pay attention to the structure of the sentence after the conjunction. Is it followed by a verb, noun or pronoun?

1 <u>Even though</u> being a top student throughout the year, he failed all his end-of-year exams. ....

2 I am going to play football every week <u>while</u> I can get fit and healthy. ....

3 <u>Meanwhile</u> Shelly was waiting in the car park, her sister was already walking home. ....

4 <u>So that</u> play on these tennis courts, you must be a member of the club. ....

5 This is my favourite video game ever. <u>Although</u>, I didn't buy the second one in the series as it was too expensive. ....

6 <u>Whereas</u> the fact that Damien usually stays at home in the evenings, they invited him to come to the cinema. ....

Useful language Prepositions of time

3 Complete the sentences with a preposition from the box. You will need to use some prepositions more than once.

at	by	for	from	in	on	since	to	until

1 I was born .... 7 a.m. .... Friday 23 December .... 2004.

2 My eight-year-old cousin hates going to bed .... night .... the summer when it is still light outside.

3 You have .... Monday morning to hand in your essay.

4 I can't wait until I can go .... holiday .... the end of the month. I really deserve it!

5 The exhibition is open .... 7.30 .... 10 p.m.

6 I've been coming to this club .... three years.

7 He's been doing his homework .... he got home.

8 I hope to have graduated .... the end of the year.

Useful language More prepositions

4 Complete the sentences with a suitable preposition.

1 There are a lot of birds nesting .... the tree in the garden this year.

2 Johan spent a lovely day walking .... town, looking at all the shops and cafés.

3 My grandma gave me toast for breakfast today instead .... cereal because we didn't have any milk in the house.

4 The quickest way to the other side of the mountain is to walk .... the tunnel.

5 This weekend I am just going to relax .... home and do nothing!

6 Imran, ... with all the other passengers, breathed a sigh of relief when the plane finally landed safely.

7 Monica was not happy with her tutor's comments .... her latest assignment.

8 The coach has asked me to go and see her after practice to talk .... my recent performance.

5 Complete the text with either a preposition or a linking expression from Exercises 1–4.

For my careers class at school we had to find some information about a job we might like to do when we leave school. I might like to be a personal shopper, so I did some research **(1)** ....the internet about the job and what you have to do.

A personal shopper helps people find exactly what they are looking for. Some people often don't have the time to walk **(2)** .... a huge shop, so they tell the personal shopper to find it for them.

(3) .... some people think being a personal shopper is an easy job, I'm sure it definitely isn't. They often work under a lot of stress to find the perfect gift or item of clothing very quickly. This means they have to know what is available and where to find it.

Personal shoppers require excellent communication skills. They need to be able to talk to their clients very efficiently **(4)** .... their expectations. They also need to motivate other shop assistants to help them.

Staying fit and healthy is also important **(5)** .... keep up with a busy schedule.

I think being a personal shopper would be great for me as I love shopping and so I could combine work and pleasure.

For questions **9–16**, read the text below and think of the word which best fits each gap. Use only one word in each gap. There is an example at the beginning (**0**).

Write your answers **IN CAPITAL LETTERS on the separate answer sheet**.

Example:

0	A	R	E															

Join the Young Green Group!

If you take an interest in the environment and **(0)** .... keen to learn more about how you can

(9) .... a real difference, the Young Green Group is for you. We are a club **(10)** .... meets in

towns and cities around the country and is open to anyone **(11)** .... the ages of 11 and 16, who wants to

(12) .... involved in raising awareness of 'green' issues.

We know you've heard it all before: turn taps off **(13)** .... you're cleaning your teeth; take the bus instead

of asking for a lift; recycle, recycle, recycle! That is why this group offers **(14)** .... a little different at

our weekly meetings. You'll learn about the direct impact our lifestyles have **(15)** .... our wildlife and

environment through a series of fun yet challenging activities. We'll also put you in touch with other young people

around the globe **(16)** .... that you can find out what's happening where they live. You may even be able

to visit them!

- How long should you spend on Part 3?
- Why do you need to read the text around each question carefully?

Useful language Prefixes

1 Add a negative prefix from the box to each of the words below. You can use each prefix more than once.

| dis-   il-   im-   in-   ir-   un- |

1 relevant   2 complete   3 realistic   4 literate
5 precise   6 respect   7 lucky   8 logical
9 regular   10 agree   11 mortal   12 secure

2 Add a prefix from the box to each of the words below.

| anti-   fore-   inter-   non-   re-   sub-   tri-   under- |

1 sense   2 cooked   3 marine   4 train
5 mediate   6 angle   7 cast   8 social

3 Match the prefixes from Exercise 2 with the meanings.
1 nothing ....*non-*..........
2 below ....
3 do something again ....
4 between ....
5 not enough ....
6 against ....
7 three ....
8 before ....

4 Complete the sentences with the word in brackets and a prefix from Exercises 1 and 2. You may need to add a suffix as well.
1 The United Nations is an .... organisation based in New York. **(nation)**
2 In most countries, it is .... to drive without a licence. **(legal)**
3 I am sorry to .... you, but unfortunately there are no more vacancies for this year's marathon. **(appoint)**
4 Unfortunately, my attempt to be the youngest person to climb Mount Everest was .... **(success)**
5 I find it highly .... that he managed to win the race. He didn't go training once last month. **(probable)**
6 This revolutionary medical procedure is able to .... cells that had previously died. **(generate)**

Useful language Comparative and superlative adjectives

5 Complete the sentences using a comparative form of the word in brackets.

1 You've got a great phone, but it's far .... **(expensive)** than mine.

2 Can you play it any ....? **(loud)** I can't hear it from here.

3 I thought the piano was much .... **(easy)** to learn than the guitar.

4 For me, swimming is much .... **(interesting)** than football.

5 Now that he's got a part-time job, Thiago wears clothes that are a lot .... **(smart)**

6 My younger sister can programme a computer much .... **(good)** than I can. It's a bit embarrassing, really.

6 Complete the sentences using a superlative form of the word in brackets.

1 This is .... **(far)** I have ever travelled from home.

2 The first time I saw the sea was by far .... **(happy)** day of my life.

3 What's the .... **(peaceful)** place you have visited?

4 With 451 people, the Vatican City is .... **(populated)** country in the world.

5 I hate my laptop! It has to be .... **(slow)** computer in the world!

6 I tried to read *Ulysses* by James Joyce but I had to give up. It must be .... **(complicated)** book ever written.

For questions **17–24**, read the text below. Use the word given in capitals at the end of some of the lines to form a word that fits in the gap **in the same line**. There is an example at the beginning (0).

Write your answers **IN CAPITAL LETTERS on the separate answer sheet**.

Tip! Depending on the context, you may have to make only one change to the word, or more changes.

Don't spend too long thinking about answers you're not sure of. Complete as many answers as you can, then return to the ones that you haven't done. You may have a better idea of those answers as you become more familiar with the text.

Example:

| 0 | U | N | L | I | M | I | T | E | D | | | | | | | | |

Tetris: the most popular video game ever

There is an almost **(0)** .... number of video games on the market   **LIMIT**
today and you could be forgiven for being under the **(17)** .... that   **IMPRESS**
the best ones are those packed with special effects, requiring great technique.
Nothing could be further from the **(18)** .... The favourite game of   **TRUE**
all time is also one of the oldest and most basic: Tetris. The player has to fit a
(19) .... of shapes together on the screen. When a whole row is   **VARY**
made without gaps between the blocks, the line vanishes. Should a line remain
(20) .... , however, new blocks will build up on top of it. Once the   **COMPLETE**
screen's full, the game's over.

Anyone can play Tetris, which makes the game very **(21)** .... to   **APPEAL**
people of all ages. Scientists also believe that the game's **(22)** .... is   **POPULAR**
due to the fact that it makes our brains work with greater **(23)** ....   **EFFICIENT**
The more we play, the easier it becomes, so we carry on, **(24)** ....   **CONTINUE**
trying to beat our last high score.

Test 2 Training — Reading and Use of English Part 4

- How many sentences do you have to rewrite in Part 4?
- After you have done each question, you should read the first sentence again and the sentence you have just written. What do you need to check?

Useful language Passives

1 Complete these passive sentences with either *by* or *with*.

1 My faulty computer was replaced .... a new one in the shop almost immediately.

2 One of my favourite songs is 'Jackie' which was recorded last year .... my sister's band.

3 This teddy bear was given to me .... my favourite aunt when I was only three years old.

4 The front of the museum is being rebuilt .... a new type of concrete.

5 The fire is said to have been started .... someone who broke into the college.

6 As you can see, the new work of art has been selected .... local schoolchildren.

2 Complete the second sentence using the passive so that it has a similar meaning to the first sentence, using the word given in capitals. Use between two and five words, including the word given.

1 Has anyone taken the dog for a walk yet?

Has the dog .... yet? **BEEN**

2 John Ferrel won the game for the Lions with a penalty in the last minute.

The game .... for the Lions with a penalty in the last minute. **WAS**

3 This company launched a new app last year and it completely changed the way we communicate with customers.

A new app .... last year and it completely changed the way we communicate with customers. **WAS**

4 They were still preparing the birthday cake two minutes before the party started.

The cake .... two minutes before the party started. **WAS**

5 The judge is going to inform us of the decision tomorrow.

We .... of the decision tomorrow. **BE**

6 The students wrote this report on the problems in the canteen.

This report .... on the problems in the canteen. **BY**

For questions **25–30**, complete the second sentence so that it has a similar meaning to the first sentence, using the word given. **Do not change the word given**. You must use between **two** and **five** words, including the word given. Here is an example (**0**).

Example:

0 I haven't seen you for ages!

TIME

It has .... I saw you!

The gap can be filled by the words 'been a long time since', so you write:

Example: | **0** | BEEN A LONG TIME SINCE

Write **only** the missing words **IN CAPITAL LETTERS on your answer sheet**.

---

25 We are sorry to say that all trains have been cancelled due to the bad weather.
APOLOGISE
We would like .... the cancellation of all trains due to the bad weather.

26 I'm sure it wasn't Julie you saw at the cinema because she's on holiday.
HAVE
It .... Julie you saw at the cinema because she's on holiday.

27 I should reduce the amount of junk food I'm eating.
CUT
I need ....the amount of junk food I'm eating.

28 'It was me that ate the last piece of cake,' Sam said.
ADMITTED
Sam .... the last piece of cake.

29 I only went to Dan's party because you were going.
NOT
I .... to Dan's party if you hadn't been going.

30 We decided to go for a walk on the beach despite it being really cold.
EVEN
We decided to go for a walk on the beach .... really cold.

- How many questions do you have to answer in Part 5?
- What kind of questions are they?
- How many options do you have to choose from?

1 Read quickly through the text below by a girl called Maria. Who do you think Maria is writing about? Check your ideas with a partner.

I'm told to like him and I know I should like him, but the truth is that I don't. Not really. I could quite happily live without him, although at the same time I don't want anything bad to happen to him. I just want him to disappear.

I know that sounds terrible, but what can I do? He is always <u>begging</u> me to do things for him that I would rather not do. But he goes on and on so much that I eventually give in and do what he wants.

His powers of directing attention to himself are <u>unparalleled</u>. If nobody looks at him or says anything to him for more than five minutes, he'll do something to make sure he is the centre of attention once again.

And don't get me started on his <u>unpredictable</u> nature. One minute he wants to go for a walk, the next he wants to sit on the sofa and eat. It is all but impossible to please him.

Despite his <u>irritating</u> features, he is one of the family, I guess. And if anyone from outside the family says something bad about our four-legged friend, I would defend him to the end!

2 You will often be asked to guess the meaning of a difficult word. Look at the word 'begging' in the second paragraph and answer as many of the following questions as you can. You won't be able to answer all the questions about this word, but this is a useful process to help you find the meaning of many words.

1 What part of speech is it (noun, verb, adjective, adverb)?

2 Is the context positive or negative?

3 What's the root of the word? Are there any prefixes or suffixes?

4 Does another word or phrase nearby help you to work out the meaning?

5 If you're still not sure, can you guess and move on to the next question?

3 Answer the following items, using the questions in Exercise 2 to help you.

1 What does *begging* mean?

   a physically attacking someone   **b** asking for something

   c shouting   **d** annoying someone

2 What does *unparalleled* mean?

   a exceptional   **b** the worst   **c** competitive   **d** afraid

3 What does *unpredictable* mean?

   a demanding   **b** changeable   **c** constant   **d** boring

4 What does *irritating* mean?

   a generous   **b** loyal   **c** persuasive   **d** annoying

Tip! For this type of question, all the options will be the same part of speech as the unknown word.

You are going to read a magazine article about a girl who took part in a TV cooking competition. For questions **31–36**, choose the answer (**A, B, C** or **D**) which you think fits best according to the text.

Mark your answers **on the separate answer sheet**.

A MEMORABLE EXPERIENCE

Sara Adelardi, 17, tells us about taking part in a TV cooking competition.

Since I was a child who stood in my grandmother's kitchen sniffing the delicious smell of freshly baked bread and homemade soups, I've known there is only one thing I want to do in life: cook. So, when I spotted an advert on a website inviting young people to apply for a TV cooking competition, there was little doubt I'd be first in line to take part. I thought 'This could be the beginning of my cooking career!'

The application process was far from straightforward, as I soon discovered. First, I had to fill in a lengthy form, detailing everything from how I became interested in cooking (that was the easy part), to things like what I hoped to get out of being part of the show (these were much trickier!). Once I'd got through that stage of the process, the next step was to cook a test dish for the show's judges: scary but exciting, too. If that was good enough, I'd be invited to take part in the four-week televised competition. One person, selected by the judges, would be voted out of the competition in each programme, until the winner was announced during the final.

Until I had to create a test dish, I'd been pretty positive about my cooking ability; I often cooked big meals for my family at the weekends, and my friends loved the little snacks I took into school for break times. But suddenly I found myself up against 11 other young people who'd been cooking for longer. Some of them – I'd known this might be the case – had even had part-time jobs as waiters, surrounded by top-class food prepared by professional chefs. Would I really be able to compete? As I stood at my counter in the test kitchen, ready to start cooking, I remembered my grandmother's advice: 'Stick to what you know best'.

The judges tasted each test dish, made a few notes, and sent us all home. Then the wait began. Had I made it to the televised competition? Eventually, the phone call came. I'd be in the first live programme of the series the following week! Our first challenge would be to make a meal with a selection of ingredients chosen by the judges.

It was impossible to know what they'd pick in advance, and I knew I'd just have to use my creativity on the day, but I was still desperate to do some preparation, and rushed straight to my parents' kitchen, pulling everything from the cupboards in a panic. All day I experimented with new flavour combinations, testing them out on my parents and sister. Most things they liked, some they didn't. What if the judges weren't keen on my dishes?

The day of the first programme dawned and suddenly there I was with the other competitors, waiting to be given our instructions. The lights were hot in the TV studio, but although I'd expected to be nervous about being filmed for a TV show, my excitement soon took over. I recognised all the ingredients spread out on the table in front of me and I was eager to get to work. I knew exactly what I was going to cook! My grandmother's words rang in my ears again. 'Keep it simple,' I thought, as I started chopping.

I didn't make it any further in the competition. The judges liked my dish and said I showed promise as a cook, but the other competitors were better on the day. I'd learnt a lot from seeing how they worked, and how imaginative their dishes were compared to mine, so I wasn't too disappointed. It had been a memorable experience, and *line 72* confirmed in my mind that cooking was the career for me. Years of learning still lie ahead of me, but one day I'd love to own my own restaurant – and help other young people fulfil their dreams too!

31 What is the writer's purpose in the first paragraph?

  A   to highlight the writer's relationship with her grandmother
  B   to describe the kinds of meals that the writer enjoyed cooking
  C   to help readers identify with the writer's ambitious character
  D   to explain why the competition appealed to the writer

32 What does the writer say about applying for the competition in the second paragraph?

  A   It took much longer than she had hoped it would.
  B   She found it challenging to answer some of the questions.
  C   The process was as complicated as she had expected it to be.
  D   She discovered details about the competition which she did not like.

33 How did the writer feel after she met the other competitors for the first time?

  A   confident that she had the necessary skills to do so
  B   determined to use the advice that she had been given
  C   concerned that they would be better at cooking than she was
  D   surprised by how much experience some of them had

34 When it was confirmed that the writer would be taking part in the televised competition, she

  A   decided to practise making some of her favourite recipes.
  B   knew there was little point trying to guess what she'd have to do.
  C   asked her family to make suggestions about what she should cook.
  D   felt she ought to find out about ingredients she didn't ordinarily use.

35 On the first day of the competition, the writer says she felt

  A   keen to get on with the task before her.
  B   anxious about appearing on camera.
  C   relieved to have ideas about what to cook.
  D   grateful for the family support she had received.

36 What does *it* refer to in line 72?

  A   the judges' feedback
  B   her time at the studio
  C   other competitors' food
  D   a feeling of disappointment

- What do you have to do in each paragraph of the Part 6 text?
- What are some examples of things to look out for when trying to find sentences that fit the gaps?

1 Read through the text below and decide which title is the best.

    a What actors want

    b The future of Hollywood

    c The dawn of a golden age of TV

> **Tip!** Remember to look for synonyms, pronouns and other referencing devices to help you choose the right sentence for the gap.

It used to be that the biggest stars, and the big money, were drawn to the cinema. The best actors were attracted to Hollywood by the glamour and the fame, and the opportunity to work with other legendary figures. <u>Many</u> were also keen on the lifestyle that was associated with life as a Hollywood star. **1**   <u>However</u>, there has recently been a major change with the biggest names in acting being as likely to appear on a TV show as in the cinema. There are many reasons for <u>this</u>, including a growth of cable TV companies eager to produce their own content, a reduction in costs associated with producing quality TV and a move away from Hollywood and California. Whatever the reasons, <u>both</u> critics and audiences agree that TV is enjoying its best time ever.

2 Look at the underlined words in the text in Exercise 1 and answer the questions.

  1 *Many* refers to

    a legendary figures.

    b best actors.

  2 *However* is used to show

    a a contrast.

    b a reason.

  3 *This* refers to

    a the growth of cable TV companies.

    b a big change.

  4 *Both* refers to

    a TV and Hollywood.

    b critics and audiences.

3 Which sentence best fits the gap in the text? Why do the other two sentences not fit?

  A The endless parties, the fashionable clothes and the constant sunshine appealed to them.

  B I know that I would like to live like that as well if I had the chance.

  C They don't seem to be so interested in showing off their wealth nowadays.

You are going to read a newspaper article about a teenage boy who writes a blog about films. Six sentences have been removed from the article. Choose from the sentences **A–G** the one which fits each gap (**37–42**). There is one extra sentence which you do not need to use.

Mark your answers **on the separate answer sheet**.

How to write a good blog

Joey Benson started writing a blog at the age of thirteen. Here, he tells us about his own experiences of blog writing and offers tips for other young bloggers starting out.

'I never expected to get many followers when I started writing my blog,' says Joey Benson, now 15. 'I just wrote down my thoughts about films I'd seen at the cinema. I didn't think anyone would take my opinions seriously or even be particularly interested in them.'

Since he started blogging two years ago, however, Joey's attracted tens of thousands of readers, some of them professional film critics, who are interested in his fresh approach to reviewing films. **37** This attention has led to him tripling the number of hits his blog receives, and he now gets sent free tickets for screenings of new films for his age group.

Joey's style is informal and chatty, and he presents an interesting angle on the films he sees. Instead of simply commenting on how amazing the special effects are, or how effective the sound track is, Joey delves into psychological subject matter like what it was that made the bad guy turn bad or whether the heroes of the story have hidden motives. **38** Why did they choose that camera angle to shoot that scene from? Why was that particular animation process selected?

Joey has certainly made an impact on the teenage and film critic blogging scenes. His ideas are far from predictable, and he never fails to surprise readers with a new take on old themes. **39** It's definitely something he manages, though.

With so many talented bloggers out there, how does Joey stand out from the crowd? He says it's crucial to either find something no one's written about before or a new way of approaching a subject, like he does. You don't have to present a balanced opinion of an issue. **40** They probably won't come back again, either.

If you're hoping to reach a wide range of readers with your blog, following advice from experienced bloggers like Joey is a wise move. You may be truly passionate about a subject close to your heart, and may even consider yourself a bit of an expert on it. This makes it tempting to use jargon and technical words that people familiar with the field will know. **41** This means you automatically limit the number of hits you receive on your blog.

'Remember the expression "first impressions count"?' asks Joey. 'Well, that doesn't just stand for meeting people but when aiming to make an impact with your blog-writing too. **42** Then keep their interest by addressing them personally, asking questions and making them think.'

One last word from Joey: 'Don't try too hard to use big fancy words or get too hung up on things like grammar. It's important to check your work afterwards for things like spelling errors, though, and make sure it flows well and is relevant to your target readers. Oh, and make sure you check your facts! You don't want to get into trouble about what you've written. Good luck!'

A Draw the reader in by writing a funny or surprising title.

B He makes it seem easy, but not all young, or indeed older, bloggers hit the right tone.

C A national newspaper recently picked up on his unique style and he's since appeared in an article about teenage bloggers.

D Age doesn't matter when you're writing about something you feel strongly about.

E He isn't only interested in considering this kind of thing, but in the technicalities of film-making, too.

F However, simply repeating the same thing over again without backing up your ideas with actual examples is unlikely to make readers stick around for long.

G Be aware, though, that a general audience may not, and you may put them off by doing so.

- What kind of text do you need to read in Part 7?
- How many questions do you need to answer?
- What do you need to do in order to answer the questions?

1   Read quickly through the text about moving house, written by a boy called Amil. Then cover the text and see how much of the information you can remember.

It was all really exciting: looking at different houses, preparing to move out and finally unpacking everything in our new home. We had to move because my mum got a new job on the other side of the city and she was spending about two or three hours a day commuting. The new house is about the same size as our old one, but it has a much bigger garden, so I persuaded my dad to get us a cat. I chose my bedroom and said I wanted it to be painted blue and white with pictures of my favourite rock bands on the walls. I miss my friends from my old school. I still see them occasionally, but not every day like I used to. I have started to make new friends, but it isn't the same.

2   Look at the text again. Underline the parts that show you the answers to the following questions.

 Tip! Identify and underline key words in the text to help you match them with the questions.

   1   Why did the family move house?

   2   What was the result of having a larger garden?

   3   What decorations does Amil have in his room?

   4   What problem does he face?

3   Now read quickly through this second text about moving house, written by a girl called Sarah. Underline the parts that show you the answers to the following questions.

I wasn't fond of the idea of moving to a new flat. I loved the old one and didn't see why we had to move at all. It was a lot of stress for my parents, but my sister and I only needed to organise our new rooms, so it wasn't a problem for us. The day of the move itself was during the week, so we went to school from one place and went home to another one. We still go to the same school and we see the same people every day, which is good because I would have missed all my friends. My bedroom is smaller, but it has a view over a park which is nice and relaxing when I do my homework.

   1   Did Sarah want to move?

   2   What did she have to do?

   3   Did she have to make new friends?

   4   What's her new bedroom like?

4   Answer these questions about both texts.

   Which person (Amil or Sarah)

   1   talks about why they moved?

   2   moved a long way from their school?

   3   wasn't involved with the move?

   4   wanted their bedroom decorated?

You are going to read an article about four teenagers who have learnt a useful life lesson. For questions **43–52**, choose from the teenagers (**A–D**). The teenagers may be chosen more than once.

Mark your answers **on the separate answer sheet**.

Which teenager

explains how admiring another person led to him accepting his own personality?	**43**	
mentions how acquiring a new skill has made him approach other things in a similar way?	**44**	
shared his hopes with someone else?	**45**	
has had a positive impact on other people's lives?	**46**	
admits to still having the same wishes for the future?	**47**	
felt frustrated that he hadn't done something he felt he should have done?	**48**	
made efforts to fit in with his classmates?	**49**	
took note of someone else's experiences of life?	**50**	
admits to struggling with something that is expected of him?	**51**	
acted on some advice he was given?	**52**	

Lessons for life

A Ben

Making mistakes is something I've always tried to avoid. I used to feel pretty terrible if I thought I'd offended someone by saying the wrong thing, or if I messed up some schoolwork because I'd rushed it. If you do something wrong, you know you're meant to acknowledge it, and I do, even though I find that tough! Anyway, last month I started going to a Chinese class in the village where I live. I don't find Chinese easy to learn quickly; for a start, there's a whole new writing system to memorise, as well as unfamiliar pronunciation and grammar. If I'd sat in the classes and not said anything because I was afraid to make mistakes, I wouldn't have learnt anything. I've also realised I can apply that to other parts of my life, too, and I do.

B Ali

I've always been ambitious – I want to be top of every class, captain of the football team, get a great job and earn loads of money when I finish school. I told my grandma about my plans one day and she said, 'What if that doesn't happen? Does that mean you'll never be happy?' That made me think. My grandparents don't live in a big house and they don't have a car. They don't have a ton of money either. Yet, they love life. I asked Grandma her secret. 'Well, I'm not interested in material things,' she said. 'Look around you. Smell those beautiful flowers, feel that sunshine on your back, laugh at Grandad's silly jokes. Don't let go of your dreams,' she advised me, 'but don't be disappointed if things don't quite work out the way you want them to.' I'm still just as ambitious and tough on myself. My character hasn't changed, but now I appreciate the smaller things in life too.

C Nathan

Being shy, like I was as a little kid, isn't great. You see the confident kids at school happy to speak up in class, taking all the best roles in school plays and just generally not being too worried by what other people think of them. I used to think being shy meant I was boring, or didn't have anything very interesting to say. I wished I could be different and tried so hard to be more outgoing or think of stuff to talk about, that I'd come home from school feeling exhausted every day. Then a new boy joined our class. He was quiet and didn't contribute much to conversations, but when he did speak, he was full of amazing ideas and didn't seem bothered by anyone disagreeing with him. That was great. He wasn't in the least concerned about whether people liked him or not either, and I learnt an important life lesson from him: just be yourself.

D Jan

The greatest lesson I've learnt is not to be afraid to ask for help. If you're struggling with something at school and everyone else seems to get it, it can be hard to ask the teacher to explain it again. I used to worry everyone would tease me about it. Then I got a bad mark for a project I did and I knew that if I'd just asked for clarification on what we were supposed to do, I could've done well. Next time there was something I didn't understand, I waited till the end of the class and asked the teacher about it. He said he wished I'd ask in class and then he could explain things better if necessary. He said maybe other students got confused too. So, next time, I spoke up. No one laughed and afterwards one or two people even thanked me – they'd been worried about asking too.

You have to answer the question in Part 1 of the writing paper. Unlike in Writing Part 2, there is no choice here.

- What do you have to write in Part 1?
- Who are you writing the essay for?
- What do you have to include?
- How many words do you have to write?

1 Read the instructions for a Part 1 question below. What is the general topic of the essay?

> In your English class you have been talking about smartphones and social networking. Now your English teacher has asked you to write an essay.
>
> Write an essay using **all** the notes and giving reasons for your point of view.

2 Work with a partner. The phrases in the box can be used for talking about digital technology. Match the phrases from the box with their definitions.

big data	cyberbullying	hacking	identity theft
location tracking	peer pressure	personalised adverts	privacy settings

1 Using information, such as phone signals, to know where a person is all the time.
2 Ways to control who can see particular information about you.
3 Advertising that is different for each person, e.g. it contains your name.
4 Very large amounts of information that can be analysed by computers to reveal patterns and trends.
5 A crime where somebody pretends to be you.
6 Breaking into a computer network, e.g. by stealing somebody's password.
7 Using the internet to hurt or frighten another person.
8 The feeling that you have to do something because your friends do.

3a Now read the essay question and the notes below.

> **Our smartphones have increasing amounts of personal information about us. What are the advantages and disadvantages for teenagers?**
> **Notes**
> Write about:
> 1. social networking
> 2. advertising
> 3. .... (your own idea)

Tip! Most Part 1 tasks provide a statement and ask if you agree with it. But other question types are also possible. For example, you might be asked about advantages and disadvantages, as in this task.

b Make notes of some advantages and disadvantages of the first two ideas.

c What could you use for the third idea? Use the phrases in Exercise 2 to help you.

Focus Discussing advantages and disadvantages

4 Read the essay that a student called Vicky wrote for her answer.

Our phones learn more and more about us from the information we provide. But what are the hidden risks of smarter smartphones?

Most people use social networking sites and messaging apps to share personal information and photos. This helps us to enjoy positive relationships with friends. However, it also exposes us to dangers like identity theft and cyberbullying.

Websites and apps need to make money, so we generally accept adverts as the price you pay for of a free app. One advantage of big data is that our phones only show us personalised adverts for things we're interested in. On the other hand, it is worrying that our phones encourage us to spend money.

Our phones track our location all the time. Apps use this information to send notifications based on where we are. While these are often helpful, such as a map showing us how to find the nearest lift, they may also be manipulative, for example an advert for a product in the shop where we are.

Overall, smartphones have some serious disadvantages. However, I believe that the benefits outweigh the drawbacks. We can always turn off tracking and notifications, and ignore adverts.

5a Did Vicky mention advantages and disadvantages for all three points? How did she do it?

b Complete the table with words and phrases that Vicky used to show advantages and disadvantages.

	Advantages	**Disadvantages**
Nouns:		*the hidden <u>risks</u>*
Verbs:	*this <u>helps</u> us to <u>enjoy</u> …*	
Adjectives:	*<u>positive</u> relationships*	

c Look at the last paragraph. What verb did Vicky use to show that there are more advantages than disadvantages?

6a Look at the essay question in Exercise 3a again. Did Vicky include all the information? What did she miss?

b How could Vicky make some simple changes to her essay to include the missing information?

> **Tip!** Always read the question again after you finish writing to make sure you haven't missed anything important!

Writing • Part 1 (essay)

You **must** answer this question. Write your answer in **140–190** words in an appropriate style **on the separate answer sheet**.

Tip! Don't waste time in the exam counting every word. Instead, practise writing within the word limit before the exam.

In your English class you have been talking about robots and computers. Now your English teacher has asked you to write an essay.

Write an essay using **all** the notes and giving reasons for your point of view.

In the future, robots and computers may be able to do most things that humans do now.

What would the advantages and disadvantages be for teenagers?

Notes

Write about:

1. school

2. home

3. .... (your own idea)

Check! Have you:

☐ included everything in the notes?
☐ written about your own idea?
☐ given reasons for your point of view?
☐ written 140–190 words?

In Part 2, there may be a question asking you to write a review, for example for an English-language magazine, newspaper or website.

In a review, you:

- **describe** the thing you are reviewing
- **present** your positive and negative opinions about it
- **state** whether you would recommend it to other people
- **justify** your opinions by providing evidence
- **write** between 140 and 190 words

> **Tip!** Your review doesn't have to be about something you love or hate – it could simply be about something you've experienced.

1 Look at this list of things you might write a review for. For each review topic in the list, think of an example you could write a review about.

- an app on your phone
- a book you enjoyed
- a film you've seen recently
- an electronic device you've used
- an exhibition or event you've been to
- a holiday you've had
- an interesting place to visit
- a magazine article you've read
- a meal you've had

- a music concert you've attended
- a place to eat out
- a place where you can relax
- a programme you saw on TV
- a product that helps you with schoolwork
- a shop where you buy clothes
- a sports event you've seen
- a trip you've been on
- a website you often use

2a Read the introductions to three reviews. Which topic from Exercise 1 is each review about?

1

> One of the most popular tourist attractions in my town is the Museum of Chocolate. Recently, I was delighted to have the opportunity to visit this museum as part of a school trip. Unfortunately, it failed to live up to my expectations.

2

> If you are looking for a place to eat good, simple Italian food at a reasonable price, I can strongly recommend Luigi's Trattoria. I have been eating here regularly with my family since I was a child, and have never been disappointed with the food or the service.

3

> I recently attended the Future Tech event in my city, where customers have the chance to try the latest technological innovations before they become available in shops. I saw many amazing devices while I was there, but by far the most memorable was a next-generation headset.

b Do you expect these reviews to be generally positive or negative? What do you think the writers of each review will say next?

Focus Sentence frames

3a A sentence frame is a model sentence, where you can change different parts to suit your needs. Look at these sentence frames from the examples above.

Tip! Get into the habit of looking for and writing down useful sentence frames that you read. Then you can use these sentence frames in your own writing.

1 One of [my/the + superlative adjective] is [place/thing].

2 Recently, I was [adjective] to have the opportunity to [verb].

3 If you are looking for a place to [verb], I can strongly recommend [place].

4 I recently attended [event], where [something happens].

5 I saw many [things] while I was there, but by far the [superlative adjective] was a [thing].

b Think of at least two other ways of completing each sentence frame for some of the ideas you thought of in Exercise 1.

4a A review should focus on three or four aspects of the thing you are reviewing. For example, a film review might focus on the following:

- the plot
- the special effects
- the quality of acting

Tip! Most reviews end with a recommendation. It is important to remember who you are making a recommendation for. For example, a wonderful restaurant for families might not be suitable for businesspeople! Remember to justify your recommendation.

b Match these aspects of reviews with the example questions.

1	convenience	a	Do the staff treat you well?
2	location	b	Does it look beautiful?
3	customer service	c	How useful is it?
4	practical value	d	Could a disabled person use it?
5	enjoyment	e	Is it worth the money you have to pay?
6	quality	f	Can you use it at a time/place that suits you?
7	user experience	g	Is it in a nice place? Is it easy to get there?
8	accessibility	h	How much fun is it?
9	value for money	i	Is it well-made?
10	attractive design	j	Is it easy to use?

c Choose four possible review topics from Exercise 1. For each topic, think of three aspects to focus on.

5 Use the table to make a recommendation for each of the review topics you have chosen.

I would strongly recommend this [what?]		families with small children		it has a good mix of [what?] and [what?].
I would not recommend this [what?]		young people		there isn't enough [what?].
This [what?] is suitable / unsuitable / appropriate / inappropriate / perfect / ideal	for	people who are looking for [what?]	because	of the [adjective + noun].
Overall, I think this [what?] is too / very [adjective]		people who love [what?]		it is the best [what?] in the city.
Unfortunately, this [what?] isn't [adjective] enough		fans of [what?]		[what?] is simply too [adjective].

Example: *Overall, I think this film is unsuitable for families with small children because there isn't enough humour.*

6a Read the exam task below.

You see this announcement on an English-language website for teenagers.

> Have you read a book that changed the way you think? Write a review telling us about the book and what effect it had on you. Would you recommend this book to other people your age? We will post the best reviews on the website!

Write your **review**.

b Now read the review that a student called Adam wrote for his answer and find:

1 Adam's recommendation
2 two sentence frames that you could use in your writing
3 three aspects that Adam focuses on

SOPHIE'S WORLD

One of the most thought-provoking books I have read is *Sophie's World*, by Jostein Gaarder. It uses the story of a 14-year-old girl called Sophie to explore 3,000 years of philosophical thought.

The story starts with Sophie finding some mysterious messages and trying to work out what they mean and where they are coming from. As the book progresses, it sometimes feels less like a story and more like a philosophy course. I found this frustrating at first, but by the end I really appreciated the deep understanding of philosophy that I acquired.

The book is written in an accessible and engaging style for teenagers. Although it covers some complicated ideas, the story helps us to understand them. The characters feel believable, and most teenagers will find it easy to identify with Sophie.

I can honestly say that this book has changed the way I think. I strongly recommend it for older teenagers who are interested in deep questions about life. However, if you are looking for a light story to entertain you, this isn't the book for you.

Test 2 Exam practice — Writing • Part 2 (review)

You see this announcement on an English-language website for young people.

Film reviews wanted!

Have you seen a film that taught you something new? Write a review telling us about the film and what you learnt from it. Would you recommend this film to other people your age?

We will post the best reviews on the website.

Write your **review**.

Check! Have you:

☐ given your review a title?   ☐ included your own opinions?
☐ included points which will interest your readers?   ☐ made your recommendation?
    ☐ written between 140 and 190 words

In Part 2 there may be a question asking you to write an article.

In an article you:

- **present** your opinions, experiences and ideas
- **engage** your readers with a lively, interesting style
- **write** between 140 and 190 words

1 Are these statements about articles or essays? Choose the options which are about articles.

1 You are writing to *a teacher / the readers of a magazine or website*.

2 You can use *a standard paragraph-by-paragraph pattern / paragraphs more creatively*.

3 You should use *a friendly and informal / an academic or neutral* style.

4 You should focus on *keeping the readers interested / building strong arguments*.

5 You want your readers to say *'Yes, that makes sense!' / 'Wow!'*.

 Tip! Always think about your target reader. In most cases, you'll be writing an article for people of your own age and with similar interests. But read the instructions carefully to make sure.

2 Read the exam task carefully and answer questions 1–3 below.

You see this notice in an English-language magazine for teenagers.

> We are looking for articles to help our readers to be better organised. How do you make sure you never forget what you need to do? How do you avoid losing important things? Do you use technology to help you?
>
> Write an article telling us about your experiences and your tips!
>
> The best articles will appear in our magazine.

Tip! Try to think of a real person who would want to read your article. For example, maybe you have a friend who is disorganised. Imagine having a conversation with that friend. This will help you make your article more natural and engaging.

Write your **article**.

1 Who are you writing the article for?

2 Why would somebody want to read your article?

3 What three things do you need to mention in your article?

3 Read an article that a student called Olivia wrote for this task. Has she included all three points from the question?

> I used to be one of the least organised people in the world. I was constantly forgetting homework and losing worksheets. The worst time was when I forgot about an important test, and turned up completely unprepared. That was when I realised I needed to change.
>
> So I bought a small diary to write down homework tasks. It's tied to my schoolbag, so I never leave it at home.
>
> Now I know what you're thinking: why not just make a note on your phone? Well, we're not allowed to use phones during lessons. Also, whenever I look at my phone, I tend to get distracted by messages. So a pen and paper works better for me.
>
> Next, I set up a 'to-do' folder on my laptop, where I save new worksheets each day. At the end of each week, I always move my old worksheets into a 'done' folder, so I know what work is completed. It's a five-minute job, but it saves time and stress later.
>
> Being organised doesn't need much time or special skills. You just need to get some good habits. And stick to them!

Useful language Past and present habits

4a Read the advice about past and present habits. Find examples of each in Olivia's article.

1 We use the structure *tend to* + infinitive for present habits. It has a similar meaning to 'usually'.

2 We use the structure *used to* + infinitive for past habits and long-term past states. It usually means that the habit/state has finished now.

3 We can use *whenever* instead of *when*. It means 'every time when'.

4 We use words like *always, usually* and *never* with the past simple or present simple to describe past and present habits.

5 We can use words like *always* or *constantly* with the past continuous or present continuous to describe bad habits that we want/wanted to stop.

> **Tip!** In your article, you often have to give advice based on your experiences. Don't worry if you're not an expert or a perfect student! In fact, it's much more interesting if you show that you're a normal person who has learnt from past mistakes.

b Rewrite these sentences using the word in brackets. Make any other necessary changes to the sentences.

1 I used to leave my pens at home, which was annoying. **(leaving)**

   Example: *I was always leaving my pens at home.*

2 Now my pen is tied to my bag, so I always have it with me. **(never)**

3 Every time I get some writing back, I save it in my 'done' folder. **(whenever)**

4 I don't get stressed very often these days. **(tend)**

5 I always got bad marks in tests. **(used)**

6 But now I tend to get better marks. **(usually)**

7 My friends always ask me what the homework is, which is a little annoying. **(constantly)**

> **Tip!** It's good to use a mixture of structures in your writing. If you over-use one structure, it doesn't sound natural.

5a Look back at Olivia's article. What technique has Olivia used to create the impression that she is having a conversation with a friend?

b Match these techniques with the examples from Olivia's article.

1 Exaggerate: pretend something is more extreme than it really is.

2 Tell a story: start by describing a bad situation.

3 Tell a story: describe a big decision.

4 Tell a story: what action did you take?

5 Talk to the reader: imagine what your reader is thinking.

6 Talk to the reader: imagine a question that your reader might ask.

7 Talk to the reader: use conversational words like *now, well* and *anyway*.

8 Talk to the reader: give advice using 'you'.

a That was when I realised I needed to change.

b So I bought a small diary to write down homework tasks.

c Why not just make a note on your phone?

d Well, we're not allowed to use phones during lessons.

e I used to be one of the least organised people in the world.

f You just need to get some good habits.

g The worst time was when I forgot about an important test …

h Now I know what you're thinking …

Follow the instructions below.

Write your answer in **140–190** words in an appropriate style **on the separate answer sheet**.

Tip! Underline the key information that you need to include in your answer. Think of examples for each point.

You see this notice in an English-language magazine for teenagers.

Helping the environment

Many young people try to protect the environment by recycling. How important is it to do this? Are there other things that people and their families should do to help the environment?

Write an article giving us your opinions!

The best articles will appear in our magazine.

Write your **article**.

Check! Have you:

☐ included all the points from the question?

☐ tried to engage your target reader?

☐ used a range of structures to describe past and present habits?

☐ written 140–190 words?

- How many short recordings do you have to listen to in this part?
- How many times do you hear each recording?
- What kind of question do you need to answer about each recording?

1a Look at the adjectives below. When was the last time you felt this way? Discuss with a partner.

> disappointed   frustrated   surprised

b Can you think of a synonym and antonym for each adjective?

2a You hear two students talking about a language learning app. Read their conversation.

> **Boy:** How did you get on with the app you downloaded?
>
> **Girl:** Oh it was great for learning some short words and phrases. It also helped with pronunciation because I could hear clearly what I was supposed to sound like.
>
> **Boy:** Yeah, that's really important.
>
> **Girl:** The only issue was that it didn't have enough different things to do. It was OK for learning phrases, but not for much else.
>
> **Boy:** That must've been hard enough, though.
>
> **Girl:** Not really. I wrote them on little notes and put them up all over the house. That way I felt like I was always practising.

b Now look at the options. How did the girl feel about the app she downloaded?

A She was delighted with it.

B She was slightly disappointed with it.

C She thought it wasn't very helpful.

c 🎧17 Listen to the recording and check your answer.

> **Tip!** In Part 1 tasks, you will often be asked to recognise how people feel. Listen for adjectives and phrases which express feeling and think of some synonyms and antonyms for them.

🎧18 You will hear people talking in eight different situations. For questions **1–8**, choose the best answer (**A**, **B** or **C**).

Tip! You will hear the context sentence, but **not** the question that follows. Read the question and the options quickly before you listen to the recording.

1   You hear a girl phoning her friend.
     What is the girl doing?

     A   apologising for something that she's lost
     B   suggesting a change in arrangements for something
     C   making an excuse for having to cancel something

2   You hear a boy talking about a football match he has just played in.
     How did he feel about the match?

     A   The result wasn't what he'd expected.
     B   The opposing team was better than he'd anticipated.
     C   The support of the crowd came as a surprise.

3   You hear two students talking about a presentation they attended by a famous author.
     What do they agree?

     A   They have a new understanding of the author's books.
     B   The author's broad experience gives his stories their appeal.
     C   The author's interest in his audience was impressive.

Advice

2 The boy says he **hadn't realised** something. What was it?

6 The girl says she **wouldn't have tackled** something. What is she talking about?

4   You hear a girl and her father talking about a restaurant menu.
     What do they agree about it?

     A   The range of dishes is limited in some respects.
     B   There are the kind of dishes they expected to find.
     C   It includes some dishes they've never tried before.

5   You hear an architect talking about a recent project he worked on.
     How did he feel during the project?

     A   inspired by the design possibilities that were available to him
     B   proud to be involved in creating a city of the future
     C   disappointed at the loss of some historical buildings

6   You hear a girl talking about her cousin, Jake.
     She describes him as someone who

     A   has always supported her when she's had problems.
     B   gave her the confidence to attempt what she's achieved.
     C   is able to give her practical help when she needs it.

7   You hear a maths teacher telling his students about a new book.
     He is recommending it because he believes it will

     A   be visually beautiful enough to maintain interest.
     B   inspire even people who aren't very interested in maths.
     C   encourage some of them to think more deeply about maths.

8   You hear a girl telling a friend about a family boating trip on the river.
     What did she see as a problem?

     A   Some of the participants wouldn't cooperate.
     B   Important supplies got left behind.
     C   They managed to get lost.

- How many people will you hear speaking in this part of the test?
- How many words might you need to write in each gap?
- How many questions will you need to answer?

1a 🎧 19 **You will hear a boy called Adam talking about a period of work experience he did in his school holidays.**

We found out halfway through the school year that we needed to do two weeks' work experience during the summer. Our teachers said that it would be an ideal way for us to find out more about the world of work, to see what it was like to have a job and to get an idea of what we wanted to study at university.

At first some of my friends were annoyed when they found out that they'd be working for free! However, our teachers explained that because it was a school project, the companies wouldn't be allowed to pay wages – the important thing was what we'd get out of the experience. So, I decided that I'd try to find something I really wanted to do. A friend of my dad's works for a TV and film production studio, which I thought would be a great place to work, so I gave him a call and asked if there was any chance of doing my work experience there. I was shocked when he said yes! There was a new movie which was being filmed at a studio not far from me, and they were happy to have some help.

So there I was, all set up for my first day. My initial thoughts were that it was the total opposite of what I imagined. It was more like a warehouse than a glamorous movie studio. It was full of builders rather than actors or camera crew. Everyone seemed to be busy fixing things. I started to think that maybe working in films wasn't what I thought it would be!

---

b **Now find the exact word or phrase to complete the sentences below.**

Some of Adam's friends were disappointed not to get any
(1) .... during their period of or work experience.
At the studio Adam was surprised to see so many (2) ....
working there.

> **Tip!** Read the sentence with the gap to identify if you need to put one word or a phrase in it. When you're listening, listen for the exact word or phrase which fits in the gap.

2a **Match these adjectives with nouns to make collocations which were used in the recording.**

1	ideal	**a**	thoughts
2	initial	**b**	way
3	total	**c**	movie studio
4	glamourous	**d**	opposite

b **Now talk with your partner and take it in turns to use these collocations in a sentence.**

Example: *'Visiting Turkey is an **ideal way** to learn Turkish.'*

20 You will hear a girl called Julie talking about a special trip she went on for her birthday. For questions **9–18**, complete the sentences with a word or short phrase.

Tip! Read the sentences carefully. Remember – your answer must fit with what comes before *and* after the gap.

A birthday trip

Julie was hoping that her birthday surprise would be a ride in a **(9)** ....

From the air, Julie managed to catch sight of the **(10)** .... in her town when she went up in a plane.

Once they were out over the water, Julie was thrilled to look down on the **(11)** .... around the coast.

Julie and her dad went from the island's airport to the nearest **(12)** ....

Julie describes the town she visited as very **(13)** ....

Julie was pleased to get some bargains at the **(14)** .... they visited.

Julie and her dad bought a type of **(15)** .... that she hadn't tried before.

After their lunch, Julie was keen to see some **(16)** .... on display on a beach.

Julie regretted turning down the chance to do some **(17)** .... at the beach.

Julie presented her dad with a **(18)** .... to show she appreciated her day out.

Advice

11 What might Julie see on the coast below her?

14 Think about where you might find bargains.

Understanding the task

- How many short extracts do you listen to in Part 3 of the listening test?
- Will they be talking about the same topic or a different one?
- How many options do you have to choose from?

1 Work with a partner and look at the list of options below. Talk about situations in which teenagers might feel like this.

A relieved when it had ended

B underprepared before it started

C disappointed with the result

D surprised at my reaction

E terrified at the beginning

F excited during the activity

G unimpressed by the overall activity

H keen to try it again

2a 🎧 21 Read what Speaker 1 says about a sport he tried for the first time. Which of the options, A–H above is he talking about? Underline the words that give you the answer, and then listen to the recording.

> I've always been sporty – I've been playing football for ages and I started going to the gym last year, but when a friend suggested something different – a yoga class! – at first I couldn't believe what she was saying. I'd always just assumed that yoga was only for girls. But she persuaded me to try it. I didn't need to prepare anything or bring any equipment, and fortunately I wasn't the only guy in the class. Once we started, I felt so relaxed, but it was amazingly physical too. At the end I was sweating, but felt really flexible, fresh and much better. I can't wait to go again!

b Compare your answer with a partner. Which words and phrases in the recording that express similar ideas to the key words in the options?

3 Tell your partner about how you felt when you tried something new for the first time. Choose one of the options in Exercise 1, but express it using different words when you talk. Try to speak for at least 30 seconds. Your partner will try to guess which of the options you chose. Now swap roles with your partner.

🎧22 You will hear five short extracts in which teenagers are talking about performing in a school play. For questions **19–23**, choose from the list (**A–H**) what each speaker says about their experience. Use the letters only once. There are three extra letters which you do not need to use.

> **Tip!** You may find that two or three options appear to match with what you have heard, but only one answer will be correct. Does your answer completely match what the speaker says?

A   I became amazingly confident in my costume.

B   I was praised for my acting ability.

Speaker 1 ⬚ **19**

C   I had problems speaking loudly enough.

Speaker 2 ⬚ **20**

D   I was desperate to impress the audience.

Speaker 3 ⬚ **21**

E   I became discouraged during an early rehearsal.

Speaker 4 ⬚ **22**

F   I was determined not to be nervous.

Speaker 5 ⬚ **23**

G   I loved working with other people.

H   I found it hard to remember what I had to say.

> **Advice**
>
> **19** The speaker says something was **damaged**. What was it?
>
> **22** What did other actors say about the speaker?

- How many speakers are there in Part 4?
- How many questions do you have to answer? What kind of questions?

Look at the questions below and the options.

Tip! In Part 4 you will need to answer seven multiple-choice questions. The recording is quite long so you will need to listen for the specific details to answer each question.

1   What does Adam say about capybaras as pets?

A More people own them than he expected.

B They have a suitable temperament.

C It is complicated to buy one online.

🎧23 Now listen to the first part of the interview and decide which option is correct. Why are the other options not correct?

You will hear an interview with a boy who has an unusual pet.

Interviewer:	Today I'm talking to Adam, who's recently become very well known because he has an unusual pet. Tell us more Adam.
Adam:	Well, basically, it's a capybara – sort of like a large hamster. It's actually the largest rodent in the world, originally from South America. They make great pets, but you don't see that many of them.
Interviewer:	And how did you come to own such a capybara as a pet?
Adam:	My dad works as a journalist, and a few years ago we went on a trip to Venezuela. We spent a weekend with a guide checking out the local wildlife. I got the chance to hold a baby capybara. It was so calm, cute and sweet, that we started wondering if a calybara might make a good pet.
	Back home, we did some research online, and came across the website of a regulated supplier of exotic pets not too far away, who had some experience with capybaras. So we bought a young capybara, and called him Hugo.

🎧24 Now listen to the second part of the interview and choose the correct option. Are the other options contradicted or not mentioned?

2   What does Adam say about his pet's behaviour?

A Hugo has a very similar character to a dog.

B Hugo isn't as intelligent as he seems.

C Hugo remembers people he's seen before.

Interviewer:	So what is Hugo like as a pet?
Adam:	Our Venezuelan friends call capybaras the stupidest animals on the planet, but mine's quite the opposite. Hugo is as intelligent as a dog, but he won't do anything if there is nothing in it for him. He seems to recognise everyone he's ever met and behaves differently depending on how he feels about them. He's an extremely calm animal who loves affection and attention. He's always waiting for me at the door when I get back from school, ready to go out for his walk.

🎧 25 You will hear an interview with a girl called Laura Rogers, who's talking about a trip to the beach to look for signs that dinosaurs once lived there. For questions **24–30**, choose the best answer (**A, B** or **C**).

Tip! Some questions may ask you about the speaker's feelings about something.

24 What made Laura decide to go on the beach trip with her uncle?

   A She recently visited an exhibition about the area.
   B She become interested in archaeology through internet research.
   C She realised it was the best way to prepare for some schoolwork.

Advice

24 What does Laura say about creative writing?

25 Where did her uncle find the dinosaur bones?

25 When Laura's uncle showed her some real dinosaur bones, she

   A found it hard to imagine how big the creature had been.
   B was disappointed to hear they hadn't been discovered locally.
   C began to hope they'd find something similar during their beach trip.

26 Laura describes the beach they went to as somewhere that

   A attracts some unusual wildlife.
   B is known for its good weather.
   C is popular only with walkers.

27 When Laura discovered a black stone during their search for dinosaurs, her uncle

   A advised her to keep it and turn it into jewellery.
   B told her it was rare to find one of that size.
   C suggested that it might be worth some money.

28 How did Laura respond when she finally saw a dinosaur footprint?

   A She didn't immediately understand what she was looking at.
   B She regretted not knowing more about animals.
   C She couldn't imagine that an animal had once walked on the beach.

29 During their exploration of an old ship further along the coast, Laura and her uncle

   A made sure they avoided doing any damage to it.
   B tried hard not to disturb the seals in the area.
   C were aware the ground was dangerous to walk on.

30 As a result of her trip to the beach, Laura

   A thinks she has discovered a new career path.
   B is proud that she can guide others around the area.
   C wants to learn how to observe more during her walks there.

- What are the questions about in Part 1 of the Speaking test?
- Who do you speak to?
- How long does this part of the test take?
- How long should you spend answering each question?

1 🎧 26 Listen to an extract from Part 1 of a Speaking test. What two topics were the main questions about?

Focus Coping strategies

2 Complete these phrases.

another	blank	catch	forgotten	repeat	tongue	word

Tip! It's normal to be a little stressed and nervous in the test. The key is to show that you can cope with this. These phrases may help you if things don't go as planned.

1 Sorry, my mind's gone ....
2 Sorry, I've .... the word.
3 It's on the tip of my ....
4 Sorry, can you .... the question?
5 Sorry, I didn't .... the word in the middle.
6 We're very ... er ... what's the ....? OK, let me put it .... way.

1 Work with a partner. Take turns to ask and answer these questions. Ask the questions in any order.

Tip! Remember to aim for about 20–30 seconds per answer. If your answer is very short, the examiner might ask *Why?* or *Why not?* to encourage you to say a little more.

Part 1	2 minutes [3 minutes for groups of three]

Interlocutor First, we'd like to know something about you.

Holidays
- What's an interesting place in your country for tourists to visit?
- Have you had any interesting holidays with your family recently?
- Do you prefer holidays in cities or in the country?
- Which do you like best, having one long holiday or several short ones?
- Is there anywhere you'd really like to visit on holiday?

2 🎧 27 Now listen to the examiner on the recording and answer the questions. (In the real exam you may also be asked *Why?* / *Why not?*)

- How many photos do you have to talk about in Part 2 of the Speaking test?
- What two tasks are you asked to complete during your long turn?
- Why is it important to listen carefully during your partner's long turn?
- How long does this part of the test take?

1a Look at the pictures and the question on page C8. Make notes of some similarities and differences between them.

b Plan how you could link your ideas from Exercise 1a together using phrases like *while*, *whereas* and *in contrast*.

> **Remember!**
>
> Remember to use the present continuous to describe what's happening in the photos, for example whether it's snowing or not, what the people are wearing, and how they're feeling.

Useful language Describing feelings

2a Here are some adjectives for describing people's feelings. Use a dictionary to check any new words. Which adjectives could you use to describe how the people in the photos on page C8 are feeling?

annoyed	cheerful	confident	delighted
depressed	disappointed	embarrassed	enthusiastic
excited	exhilarated	fed up	frustrated
furious	impressed	nervous	playful
proud	relieved	shocked	stressed
terrified	thrilled		

b Choose the best adjectives to complete the sentences.

1 The people in the photo seem to be very *depressed / enthusiastic / stressed* about the concert – they're definitely enjoying themselves.

2 It looks like they've had some kind of accident, but as far as I can tell, nobody's injured, so they must be feeling *annoyed / nervous / relieved*.

3 The girl in the picture has just received some kind of present, but actually she looks *delighted / disappointed / enthusiastic* with it.

4 They've just won a sports competition, and they're wearing their medals. They all look very *frustrated / furious / proud*.

5 The picture shows a teenager and his parents. There's a broken vase on the floor. The teenager looks *excited / embarrassed / impressed*, perhaps it was him that broke it.

6 These people are waiting for a train, but it looks like they've been waiting a long time because they all look totally *playful / fed up / thrilled*.

7 The boy in the picture is trying to read a book, but he's *confident / frustrated / exhilarated* because the other boys are talking really loudly, so he can't concentrate.

8 It's strange because it's clearly cold and windy in the picture, but the people aren't sad at all. In fact, they all look really *cheerful / shocked / terrified*.

3 🎧28 Listen to two teenagers, Rosie and Lukas, talking about the photos on page C8. Which adjectives from Exercise 2a did they use?

Useful language Indirect questions

4a Look at these indirect questions from Rosie's long turn. What are the equivalent direct questions?

Tip! You can use indirect questions to make your long turn feel more like conversational.

1 It's hard to tell whether these two people on the right know each other or not.

Example: Do these two people on the right know each other or not? ....

2 I don't know if they're on a mountain or something.

Are ....

3 It's hard to tell how the people in the bottom picture are feeling.

How ....

4 I wonder if these people are feeling frustrated because they want to get home.

Are ....

b Change these direct questions into indirect questions.

1 How many people are there in the group?

It's hard to make out ....

2 How are the people in the picture feeling?

I can't tell ....

3 Are they excited or scared?

It's hard to see ....

4 Where have the people come from?

I don't know ....

5 Do the people want to be there?

I'm not sure ....

6 Why isn't this person sitting with the others?

I wonder ....

7 What kind of game are they playing?

It's not clear ....

8 Do the people have big bags because they are camping?

I have no idea ....

Look at the exam instructions below and photos on pages C9 and C10. Then do this exam task in pairs.

Part 2   4 minutes [6 minutes for groups of three]

Interlocutor In this part of the test, I'm going to give each of you two photographs. I'd like you to talk about your photographs on your own for about a minute, and also to answer a question about your partner's photographs.

(*Candidate A*), it's your turn first. Here are your photographs on page C9 of the Speaking appendix. They show **people using mobile phones in different situations**.

I'd like you to compare the photographs, and say **why you think the people are using mobile phones in these situations**.

All right?

Candidate A

🕐 *1 minute* ....

Interlocutor Thank you.
(*Candidate B*), **do you use your mobile phone a lot? (Why? / Why not?)**

Candidate B

🕐 *Approximately 30 seconds* ....

Interlocutor Thank you.

Now, (*Candidate B*), here are your photographs on page C10 of the Speaking appendix. They show **people reading in different places**.

I'd like you to compare the photographs, and say **why you think the people have chosen to read in these places**.

All right?

Candidate B

🕐 *1 minute* ....

Interlocutor Thank you.

(*Candidate A*), **which of these places would you prefer to read in? (Why?)**

Candidate A

🕐 *Approximately 30 seconds* ....

Interlocutor Thank you.

- Who do you speak to in Part 3 of the Speaking test?
- What are you asked to look at?
- Do you have to start speaking immediately?
- Which question **don't** you see?
- How long does this part of the test take?

Focus Understanding the task

1a Read about how the Speaking test is assessed.

There are four criteria for assessment of the Speaking test. They are equally important in your total mark.

- **Grammar and Vocabulary:** Do you use a good range of grammar structures and vocabulary? Do you use grammar and vocabulary accurately and appropriately?
- **Discourse Management:** Can you speak fluently, without too much hesitation? Do you organise and present your ideas in a logical way that makes your arguments easy to follow?
- **Pronunciation:** Do you pronounce sounds, words and sentences clearly and accurately? Is it easy to understand the way you speak?
- **Interactive Communication:** Do you work well with a partner, e.g. inviting your partner to speak and responding appropriately to what he/she says?

b Are these statements true or false?

1 Grammatical accuracy is the most important assessment criterion.

2 It's better to use simple language accurately than to take risks with more advanced language.

3 It is important to link your ideas together clearly.

4 Pronunciation is not as important as vocabulary.

5 It doesn't matter if you don't work well with your partner.

Tip! Many candidates worry too much about making grammar mistakes. In fact, grammatical accuracy is just a small part of the assessment criteria. Interactive communication is probably the easiest criterion to improve, and Part 3 is your first opportunity to show your interactive skills. Don't waste your chance to make a good impression!

Focus Interactive communication

2a What can you do if you find yourself in one of these situations?

1 Your partner speaks too much and doesn't give you a chance to talk.

2 Your partner has nothing to say.

b 🎧29 Listen to two extracts from different Speaking tests. What is the problem? What does the girl do well in each extract?

Tip! Don't panic if you find your partner difficult to work with. You won't lose marks for this. Stay calm and patient. Do your best to make the conversation as interactive as possible.

3 Match this advice with examples from the extracts.

1 It's always good to invite your partner to start the discussion.

2 If you haven't had a chance to say anything about a point, ask to go back.

3 If you haven't finished what you were saying, ask to go back.

4 If your partner is struggling to think of something to say, give him/her a few seconds to think, and then make your point.

5 When you make your point, use a question tag and your partner's name to encourage him/her to speak.

6 Ask extra questions that your partner will find easier to answer.

7 Respond positively to what your partner says.

a What's the air like where you live, Zak?

b Before we talk about books, can we talk about the internet a bit more?

c Obviously, that's really important for our health, isn't it, Zak?

d Sorry, Zak, can I just say something about the first point?

e **Zak:** It's OK. It's … er … clean.
Alice: Oh, that's good.

f What do you think, Zak?

g **Zak:** I … er … well, ….
Alice: Shall we start with the first point, fresh air?

Test 2 Exam practice Speaking • Part 3

Look at the exam instructions below and the question and ideas on page C11, then do this task in pairs.

Part 1	4 minutes [5 minutes for groups of three]

Interlocutor Now I'd like you to talk about something together for about two minutes.

Some people think it's easy to have a healthy lifestyle, and other people disagree. Here are some reasons they give and a question for you to discuss.

First you have some time to look at the task on page C11 of the Speaking appendix.

Now talk to each other about **whether it's easy to have a healthy lifestyle**.

Candidates

🕐 *2 minutes (3 minutes for groups of three)*

Interlocutor Thank you. Now you have about a minute to decide **which is the most difficult thing about having a healthy lifestyle**.

Candidates

🕐 *1 minute (for pairs and groups of three)*

Interlocutor Thank you.

- What are the questions in Part 4 of the Speaking test about?
- Do you see the questions written down?
- Do you answer the same questions as your partner?
- How long does this part of the test take?

1 🎧30 Listen to two candidates, Ines and Will being asked questions in Part 4. What topics did they discuss? Did the examiner tell the candidates who should answer each question?

Focus Responding enthusiastically

2 🎧30 Complete these sentences from the discussion with words from the box. Then listen to the discussion again to check.

> **Remember!**
> Remember to acknowledge your partner's point of view after they have spoken, e.g. *That's a great idea!* or *That's true, but ...* .

| absolutely | brilliant | exactly | excellent | incredibly | really | totally |

1 That's a .... idea.
2 You're .... right.
3 Yes, that's a .... good point.
4 Absolutely. I .... agree.
5 Yes, that's .... important.
6 Hmmm ... that's an .... question.
7 Yes, ...

Test 2 Exam practice | Speaking • Part 4

Work in pairs. Ask and answer these questions.

Part 4   4 minutes [6 minutes for groups of three]

Interlocutor

> **What do you think?**
> **Do you agree?**
> **And you?**

- How can people be encouraged to take exercise?
- Some people say it's the government's responsibility to help people understand how to be healthy. What do you think?
- Do you think it's important for everyone to be able to cook for themselves? (Why? / Why not?)
- Is it a good idea for families to eat at least one meal together every day? (Why? / Why not?)
- Is it important to read labels on food before you buy it? (Why? / Why not?)
- Do you think people lead healthier lifestyles now than in the past? (Why? / Why not?)

Thank you. That is the end of the test.

For questions **1–8**, read the text below and decide which answer (**A**, **B**, **C** or **D**) best fits each gap. There is an example at the beginning (**0**).

Mark your answers **on the separate answer sheet**.

Example:

0   **A** change   **B** difference   **C** variation   **D** contrast

0	A	B	C	D
	▭	▬	▭	▭

Child's play?

Imagine a restaurant, but with a **(0)** .... The restaurant is run **(1)** .... by children aged under 11; they cook and serve the food, and then wash up. The children even bring the bill at the end of the meal, all with a little help from the **(2)** .... staff of course. There are always four adults on hand to **(3)** .... the youngsters. There's a set menu with a main course and dessert, and everything is made from fresh **(4)** .... The food is healthy and prices are **(5)** .... and so, not surprisingly, the restaurant is very popular. This means that a reservation is usually necessary to be **(6)** .... of getting a table. The **(7)** .... idea is to help parents by providing childcare, and to help children learn to be responsible. This is done by giving them independence in a fun and child-friendly **(8)** .... Is this the stuff of dreams? No, it's the new reality of the 21st century.

1   **A** entirely   **B** all   **C** substantially   **D** thoroughly

2   **A** rising   **B** increased   **C** grown-up   **D** expanding

3   **A** command   **B** order   **C** demand   **D** supervise

4   **A** flavours   **B** ingredients   **C** courses   **D** components

5   **A** low   **B** small   **C** little   **D** minor

6   **A** sure   **B** definite   **C** truthful   **D** known

7   **A** easy   **B** elementary   **C** introductory   **D** basic

8   **A** position   **B** neighbourhood   **C** environment   **D** region

For questions **9–16**, read the text below and think of the word which best fits the gap. Use only **one** word in each gap. There is an example at the beginning (**0**).

Write your answer **IN CAPITAL LETTERS on the separate answer sheet.**

Example:

| 0 | S | I | N | C | E | | | | | | | | | | | | | |

My uncle the skateboarder

I'm 14 now, and like my mates, I really love skateboarding. I've been into it **(0)** .... I was 11. So my family have got **(9)** ....to me talking about it all the time! I knew that my dad and his brother also spent a lot of **(10)** .... teenage years riding around on skateboards, so I guess it's a family thing. My dad had to give it up when he injured his back in a fall. But **(11)** .... surprised me was finding out recently that my uncle still does it. I saw him at our annual family reunion and I couldn't believe what he was saying, especially as he's no less **(12)** .... 52 years old. He says his skateboard is his favourite **(13)** .... of getting to his office every day. He uses it in **(14)** .... to save time, which makes sense, as walking takes much longer. Plus it must be easily the **(15)** .... enjoyable form of transport. I hope I'm still doing it **(16)** .... I'm 52!

For questions **17–24**, read the text below. Use the word given in capitals at the end of some of the lines to form a word that fits in the gap **in the same line**. There is an example at the beginning (**0**).

Write your answer **IN CAPITAL LETTERS on the separate answer sheet**.

Example: | **0** | | A | L | L | O | W | E | D | | | | | | | | | | | |

Smartphones at school

Some of the schools in my home town are really strict and students

are not (**0**) .... to use their smartphones at school. Mine   **ALLOW**

is different – there's a much more (**17**) .... policy. In break   **RELAX**

times, it's (**18**) .... to use our smartphones. But in lessons,   **ACCEPT**

it's the individual teacher's (**19**) .... whether we can use   **DECIDE**

them or not. For some pieces of work, like a timed writing task,

they're completely (**20**) .... Of course it's our   **FORBID**

(**21**) .... to follow the rules, which we do. In some lessons,   **RESPONSIBLE**

the teachers actively encourage us to use our phones when they think

it'll be (**22**) .... to us. There are lots of really good ways to   **BENEFIT**

use smartphones in class, and I'm in favour of these. One example is

games, where we choose multiple-choice answers on our phones. I'm

really (**23**) .... , so love doing those. Although it can be a   **COMPETE**

bit (**24**) .... , when everyone just uses their phone instead   **SOCIAL**

of talking.

For questions **25–30**, complete the second sentence so that it has a similar meaning to the first sentence, using the word given. **Do not change the word given.** You must use between **two** and **five** words, including the word given. Here is an example (**0**).

Example:

0   I haven't seen you for ages!

TIME

It has .... I saw you!

The gap can be filled by the words 'been a long time since', so you write:

Example: | **0** | BEEN A LONG TIME SINCE |

Write only the missing words **IN CAPITAL LETTERS on the separate answer sheet**.

---

25   It's a shame I arrived late at the party.
TURNED
I wish .... late to the party.

26   Provided that you help me with my project, you can borrow my book.
LONG
I'll lend .... as you help me with my project.

27   You need to do your homework now.
TIME
It .... homework done.

28   I must get a haircut this week.
NEEDS
My .... this week.

29   It's possible that I didn't bring my books with me this morning.
MIGHT
I .... behind this morning.

30   During the lesson, I tried as hard as I could.
BEST
I .... during the lesson.

You are going to read a blog post in which a teenage boy describes his relationship with his parents. For questions **31–36**, choose the answer (**A**, **B**, **C** or **D**) which you think fits best according to the text.

Mark your answers **on the separate answer sheet**.

Teenagers and parents – it's the same old story...

Many readers have described the ups and downs of living with teenage children.
This week, we hear from Barry Davros, 15.

OK, I'll admit it. Things haven't been so easy at home in the last couple of years. I'd like to think I'm old enough and wise enough to know that it's almost certainly because I'm a teenager now. Teenagers complain to their friends about their parents. And I think we can be pretty certain that the parents do the same about their kids. I argue with mine. We don't talk as much as we did when I was a kid. It's not that this is the way I want it – I'd prefer it if we never argued, but found a way to talk about what was bothering us. That would be so much better, not just for me and my mum and dad, but for any teenager and their family. So I've been reading a lot – books like *The Teenage Brain*, and lots of online stuff. And I'm sure that if people understood more about what goes on inside a teenager's mind, half of the arguments over the dinner table wouldn't even start in the first place. So I'd like to share what I've learnt.

There are so many things that parents have a go at their teenagers for that it's almost impossible to know where to start. So let's just pick mornings. Mornings are for sleeping. For as long as you need to, or at least as long as you can. Every teenager knows that. But not parents – they think that we should get up at 7.30, just because they get up at 7.30, ready for another busy day. So who's right? Well, the science says that an adolescent's body clock isn't programmed in the same way, and is on a schedule about three hours behind that of older adults (that means both going to bed and getting up).

Another 'issue' that parents make a big deal about is tidiness. Clothes dumped on the bathroom floor, an old plate of food under the bed, house keys lost. OK, I admit, I've been guilty of all of these things recently (but at least

I owned up!). Sorting stuff like this takes planning, and the way the teenage brain develops means that it's just not our strong point. Sorry! The brain develops a chemical called myelin, and it's created over time. Until it's fully developed in all parts of the brain, it does unfortunately mean that even very bright teens can do really stupid things. So just bear with us guys!

Because as already mentioned, the teenage brain goes through all sorts of changes, sometimes teenagers can get angry. This usually makes parents angry. Which makes us angrier, which... OK, you get the picture. But parents need to understand more about what's going on inside our heads. Like, there might be a perfectly understandable (to us) reason why we don't want to do that maths homework this instant. So, listen parents out there, try and understand! Don't always respond to us by getting angry. Just don't! Calm down, count to ten and think twice.   *line 49*

Communication. That's a big one. Sure, teens and parents need to hang out together too, not live in separate worlds. But I'm 15, so the topics of conversation I was into when I was 11 don't work for me now. Same for all kids my age. The sooner parents realise that, the better. We don't stop loving   *line 54* them just because we're in our teens, it's just that we need more space. To grow up and find out who we are.

Here's a tip – if there's something that needs to be discussed, do it on a car journey. Whether it's the whole family together or just two of you, the fact that you're in a car means that you're gazing ahead, rather than staring at each other. For me, it just makes it easier to talk somehow, because I sometimes feel they're judging me or something if they're observing me. Try it. It works. And you heard it from me.

31 Why shouldn't parents be surprised if their teenagers sleep late?

    A   Many teenagers find their busy schedule tiring.
    B   Some teenagers need more hours of sleep than adults.
    C   Teenagers prefer not to see their parents in the mornings.
    D   It's natural for teenagers to have different sleep patterns from adults.

32 In the third paragraph, the writer admits that teenagers tend not to be very

    A   honest.
    B   organised.
    C   confident.
    D   intelligent.

33 What does the writer mean when he advises parents to 'count to ten' in line 49?

    A   don't react too quickly
    B   repeat what you have said
    C   find ten reasons for the behaviour
    D   don't tell teenagers things they already know

34 What does 'that' refer to in line 54?

    A   Teenagers need to spend time away from their parents.
    B   Teenagers love their parents less than they did as children.
    C   Teenagers want to talk about different things as they mature.
    D   Teenagers need to spend more time talking to their parents.

35 Car journeys are a good opportunity to speak because

    A   the speakers don't need to look at each other.
    B   the vehicle provides more privacy.
    C   families can travel somewhere nice together.
    D   teenagers cannot avoid their parents when they are in the same car.

36 Why has Barry written this blog post?

    A   to help families get along better
    B   to explain why his parents annoy him
    C   to encourage parents, doctors and teachers to read more about teenagers
    D   to suggest that it is important for teenagers to be responsible

You are going to read an article about sports shoes. Six sentences have been removed from the article. Choose from the sentences **A–G** the one which fits each gap (37–42). There is one extra sentence which you do not need to use.

Mark your answers **on the separate answer sheet**.

Sneakers

Sneakers, or shoes designed mainly for sports and other outdoor activities, are worn in almost every country in the world. Arguably they have become a symbol of globalisation itself.

Yet there are some variations, not least in what they are called. In the US, they have always been 'sneakers', at least ever since the *Boston Journal* explained it to its readers as being 'the name boys give to tennis shoes' back in 1887. **37** However, in Britain, the word 'trainers' is much more common. Other names include 'daps' and 'plimsolls', which itself dates back to the 1870s. They are also known as 'rubber shoes' in the Philippines, 'tennies' in South Africa, 'running shoes' in Australia and 'canvas shoes' in Nigeria.

During the late 19th century, sneakers were worn by holidaymakers, as well as by sports players on the tennis court. The main advantage of wearing these shoes was that they enabled the wearer to move around quickly. **38** Later designs for sports players made this even more effective by also adding metal spikes which would dig into the ground.

British company JW Foster and Sons produced the first shoes made specifically for running in 1895, and the spikes allowed for greater acceleration and speed. **39** There, runners Harold Abrahams and Eric Liddell won their 100 metre and 400 metre running races while wearing these shoes. Doubtless Foster and Sons were delighted. The fortunes of Abrahams and Liddell were memorably portrayed in the Oscar-winning 1981 film *Chariots of Fire*.

During the 1920s and 1930s, sports became associated with building moral character and raising national pride. Demand for sneakers rose as a result, so manufacturers

could afford to make the designs more varied. **40** All around the world, different shoes were also being produced

for different sports. In France, a brand called Spring Court marketed the first canvas tennis shoe, complete with eight little holes for ventilation on the side of their rubber soles.

During the 1950s, people in America and Europe began to have more free time, more leisure opportunities, and often more money to spend. There were great changes in the attitudes and habits of the new generation. **41** Previously, they had simply worn the same things as adults, but in smaller sizes. Dress codes relaxed, and fashion items from sneakers to jeans became more and more popular.

Many were interested in what people such as US pop singer Elvis Presley and sporting heroes were wearing, and then wanted the same for themselves. Now it is common for sports stars to endorse (be seen to recommend) and advertise a particular brand of sneaker: recent examples include tennis ace Roger Federer and basketball star Lebron James. But did you know that this is a long-standing tradition, and that perhaps the bestselling sports shoe ever, the Converse All-Star was endorsed by basketball player Chuck Taylor as long ago as 1923?

Sneakers continued to become more and more popular. **42** This made sneakers the cheaper option, which in turn made young people even more likely to buy them instead of an alternative which seemed old-fashioned and was more expensive.

A   This was one of the main problems with wearing sneakers.

B   This was achieved by the use of an engraved piece of rubber on the underside of the shoe, which improved grip.

C   For example, men's sneakers now became distinct from women's.

D   In fact, sales grew so much that they negatively affected sales of traditional leather footwear.

E   For perhaps the first time, children and teenagers everywhere were choosing for themselves what to wear.

F   They became very popular with athletes, including at the 1924 Olympics.

G   The term is also the standard name in Canada.

You are going to read an article about four people who achieved great things when they were teenagers. For questions **43–52**, choose from the people (**A–D**). The people may be chosen more than once.

Mark your answers **on the separate answer sheet**.

Which person

wrote a book?	43	
found a way to enable people to do something more quickly?	44	
looked older than he was?	45	
now visits other countries?	46	
chose an unexpected career?	47	
broke a record for raising money?	48	
was surprised by his own popularity?	49	
inspired other teenagers to succeed?	50	
was looked after by a well-known person?	51	
used feedback to improve an idea?	52	

Teenage success stories

A Balamurali Ambati, doctor

Balamurali Ambati was clearly very talented as a boy, studied hard at school and did well. Along with his older brother, he co-authored a medical manual aged just 11 aimed at would-be doctors. It was already obvious what he wanted to become – a doctor, and so he worked hard to achieve his dream. He graduated from New York University when he was 13, began medical school when he was 14, attending the Mount Sinai School of Medicine, also in New York. Being very tall (over 1 metre 80 centimetres), he didn't stand out as being different, and so people assumed he was the same age as the other students on his course. He graduated aged just 17, becoming the world's youngest doctor, a record which he still holds. These days, Ambati is now Professor of Neurobiology at the University of Utah, and works as a volunteer with the ORBIS Flying Eye Hospital, practising and teaching in developing nations across the globe.

B Nick D'Aloisio, computer programmer

Aged just 15, Nick D'Aloisio made headlines with the app he created, Trimit, which reduced news content into short summaries that could be processed in much less time than would be needed to process the original text. When his app received funds from Hong Kong, Nick became the youngest person ever to have received such investment. The money helped Nick to identify criticisms of Trimit from user comments, and then to redesign and rename the app as Sumly, which was released to much praise in December 2011. Since then, he has published academic articles, studied for an Oxford University degree, and continues to develop his business.

C Luka Sabbat, model

When you look at the Instagram feed of model, influencer and internet sensation Luka Sabbat, it's easy to see why he's been called 'the internet's coolest teenager'. When he started using social media, his name spread very quickly. 'For some reason, people were really into me. I don't know why' he says modestly. Even as a toddler, Luka was well connected – his babysitter was high-profile model Lara Stone. For Luka and his career, it seems that the only way is up. He models for top brands and it's not unusual for a picture of him just sitting on a chair to get over 30,000 likes in a matter of minutes. When Luka has something to say, the online world sits up and takes notice.

D Boris Becker, tennis player

The German tennis player came to the world's attention as an unknown 17-year-old when he became Wimbledon champion in London in 1985. His powerful serve, strength and speed on the court enabled him to beat the South African Kevin Curren, then ranked the world's fifth best men's player. The tennis world had never experienced such an extraordinary result. When Becker was a young teenager, becoming a sporting superstar wasn't really on the cards. 'My parents' plan for me was to finish school, go to university, get a proper degree and learn something respectable. The last thing on everyone's mind was me becoming a tennis professional.' But he turned professional at the age of 16, and the rest is history. Becker's success prompted adolescents all over the world to take up the game, hit the ball hard and try to do their very best. Becker now lives in Switzerland.

You must answer this question. Write your answer in **140–190** words in an appropriate style **on the separate answer sheet**.

1   In your English class you have been talking about school holidays. Now your English teacher has asked you to write an essay for homework.

Write your essay using **all** the notes and giving reasons for your point of view.

> **Some people say that school holidays are too long, and school students should only have a three-week break in the summer. What do you think?**
>
> **Notes**
>
> Write about:
>
>   1. how much students need to learn
>
>   2. whether having a routine is important
>
>   3. .... (your own idea)

Write an answer to **one** of the questions 2–5 in this part. Write your answer in **140–190** words in an appropriate style **on the separate answer sheet**. Put the question number in the box at the top of the answer sheet.

2   Your English teacher has asked you to write a story for the school website.

Your story must begin with this sentence:

Karen didn't wake up until ten o'clock.

Your story must include:

• a problem

• a journey

Write your **story**.

3   You have seen this announcement in an English-language magazine for teenagers.

> ***Reviews wanted!***
>
> We want to know about the technology that young people use every day. Tell us about one device that is really important to you in your daily life. What do you like about it? How could it be better? Would you recommend it to other teenagers?
>
> We will publish the best reviews next month!

Write your **review**.

4   You see this announcement on an English-language website for teenagers.

> **Articles wanted**
>
> **We want to know what sports you really love.**
>
> What sports do you enjoy watching? What's the best way to watch them?
>
> Do you think that some professional players are paid too much? Why? / Why not?
>
> The best articles will appear on our website!

Write your **article**.

5   Answer the following question based on the set text.

This is part of an email you have received from an English-speaking friend about the set text.

> Reply   Forward
>
> I enjoyed most of the book, but I thought the ending was disappointing. What did you think about the ending? If you could change the ending, how would it be different?

Write your **email**.

🎧 31 You will hear people talking in eight different situations. For questions **1–8**, choose the best answer (**A**, **B** or **C**).

1   You hear a girl telling a friend about a charity walk she went on.
     What does she say about the walk?

     A   There was an unexpected change in the weather.
     B   Some people had to give up due to injury.
     C   The route was more difficult than usual.

2   You hear a teacher talking to his class about a play they are going to see at the theatre.
     What does he want them to do?

     A   compare their impressions of the play before and after their visit
     B   carefully consider the motives of one of the characters
     C   think about whether the stage scenery is appropriate

3   You hear a girl talking about her brother's new job.
     Why did he decide to apply for it?

     A   to have a complete change from his former position
     B   to be offered the opportunity to travel
     C   to improve his promotion prospects

4   You hear a boy talking to his sister about the meal she's cooking.
     How does she respond to what he says?

     A   She objects to his criticism.
     B   She's grateful for his suggestion.
     C   She improves on his idea.

5   You hear a boy telling a friend about a toy he played with as a child.
     What does he say about it?

     A   He always felt dissatisfied with it.
     B   He made more friends because of it.
     C   His dad felt sad once he stopped playing with it.

6   You hear a girl getting advice from a friend about some creative writing homework.
     Which advice does she decide to follow?

     A   finding an alternative way of getting inspired
     B   seeking help from a reliable source
     C   taking some time out before continuing

7   You hear a teacher telling her class about an exhibition on their city's architecture.
     What does she want them to do there?

     A   consider what has influenced changes in the city's architecture
     B   decide to what extent the city has been improved
     C   come up with ideas for further changes to benefit other cities

8   You hear a boy telling his cousin about a skiing trip he went on.
     After hearing his story, his cousin

     A   admits that he would have felt the same as him.
     B   agrees that he took the right course of action.
     C   suggests that it isn't entirely true.

🎧 32 You will hear a boy called Jamie giving a talk about a family road trip he went on in the United States. For questions **9–18**, complete the sentences with a word or short phrase.

Colorado road trip

Jamie says his parents wanted to visit somewhere with a variety of **(9)** ....

At the first small town they stayed in, they had a view of a **(10)** .... from their hotel room.

Some towns they passed through had developed as a result of the **(11)** .... that had once been there.

In one town, Jamie bought some **(12)** .... , which were vintage ones.

Jamie particularly remembers some **(13)** .... that he ate on his trip.

The family were interested to see how the landscape slowly changed to **(14)** .... as they drove along.

Jamie was disappointed not to spot any **(15)** .... while they were driving.

As Jamie's mum drove them to Aspen, she was concerned about a **(16)** .... that was forecast.

In Aspen, Jamie's parents thought they should try **(17)** .... while they were there.

While swimming in their hotel pool in Aspen, the family were surprised to see a **(18)** ....

(33) You will hear five teenage writers talking about the process of creative writing. For questions **19–23**, choose from the list (**A–H**) the advice each speaker gives. Use the letters only once. There are three extra letters which you do not need to use.

A   Ask friends to read and comment on your writing.

B   Add new characters to make your writing more lively.

Speaker 1   `19`

C   Don't plan your ending too soon.

Speaker 2   `20`

D   Write at speed and then go back and improve your writing.

Speaker 3   `21`

E   Don't become discouraged when you're stuck for ideas.

Speaker 4   `22`

F   Experiment with how your writing sounds.

G   Don't get distracted while you're writing.

Speaker 5   `23`

H   Read the work of great writers for inspiration.

🎧 34 You will hear an interview with a young guitarist called Tom, whose band has just won a national music competition. For questions **24–30**, choose the best answer (**A**, **B** or **C**).

24   Tom started playing the electric guitar because

    A   he was encouraged to do so by his parents.
    B   he found certain pieces of guitar music appealing.
    C   he failed to make progress on other instruments.

25   What did Tom love about his new electric guitar?

    A   It filled him with confidence when he performed in public.
    B   It helped him make friends because he could play so well.
    C   It made him look like a rock star in his photos.

26   What did Tom realise when he started looking for a personal guitar tutor?

    A   He would prefer to be taught by a tutor online.
    B   Progress would depend on his relationship with his tutor.
    C   It would be possible for him improve quickly without a tutor's help.

27   How did Tom feel when he discovered he'd lost his guitar?

    A   furious with himself for having been so careless
    B   pessimistic about his chances of getting it back
    C   determined to replace it as quickly as possible

28   Once Tom was reunited with his electric guitar, he found

    A   the instrument looked more sophisticated than he'd remembered.
    B   it was easier than he'd thought to instantly start playing.
    C   the discomfort of playing was far less than he'd expected.

29   Tom thinks that in comparison with other instruments, the electric guitar

    A   can produce a greater volume.
    B   is easier to transport and practise on.
    C   is more suited to being played in a group.

30   What did Tom feel about the response of an audience member during the competition?

    A   put off by the way he copied Tom's actions.
    B   flattered that he was so impressed by Tom's playing.
    C   embarrassed that he valued Tom's talent so highly.

Interlocutor First we'd like to know something about you.

Everyday life

- How do you travel to school every day? (Why?)
- How much time do you spend with friends every week? (Where do you meet your friends?)
- What kind of food do you like to eat? (Why?)
- What would your perfect weekend be like?
- Have you always lived in the same house or flat as you do now? (Why? / Why not?)

Part 2 4 minutes [6 minutes for groups of three]

Interlocutor In this part of the test, I'm going to give each of you two photographs. I'd like you to talk about your photographs on your own for about a minute, and also to answer a question about your partner's photographs.

(Candidate A), it's your turn first. Here are your photographs on page C12 of the Speaking appendix. They show **people relaxing in different situations**.

I'd like you to compare the photographs, and say **what you think the people are enjoying about relaxing in these situations**.

All right?

Candidate A
🕐 1 minute ....

Interlocutor Thank you.

(Candidate B), **do you enjoy spending time outside? (Why? / Why not?)**

Candidate B
🕐 Approximately 30 seconds ....

Interlocutor Thank you.

Now (Candidate B), here are your photographs on page C13 of the Speaking appendix. They show **people taking photographs in different situations**.

I'd like you to compare the photographs, and say **why you think the people are taking photographs in these situations**.

All right?

Candidate B
🕐 1 minute ....

Interlocutor Thank you.

(Candidate A), **do you take a lot of photographs? (Why? / Why not?)**

Candidate A
🕐 Approximately 30 seconds ....

Interlocutor Thank you.

Part 3   4 minutes [5 minutes for groups of three]

Interlocutor Now I'd like you to talk about something together for about two minutes.

I'd like you to imagine that a school is deciding whether to organise a trip for students to visit another country. Here are some ideas and a question for you to discuss.

First you have some time to look at the task on page C14 of the Speaking appendix.

Now talk to each other about **what the advantages and disadvantages of a school trip to another country might be**.

Candidates

🕐 *2 minutes (3 minutes for groups of three)*

Interlocutor Thank you. Now you have about a minute to decide **which is the most important reason for organising a school trip to another country**.

Candidates

🕐 *1 minute (for pairs and groups of three)*

Interlocutor Thank you.

Part 4   4 minutes [6 minutes for groups of three]

Interlocutor

- Is it possible to have a good holiday without spending a lot of money?

- Some people say we should not travel so much because of the effect on the natural environment. Do you agree?

- Do you think there are too many school holidays or not enough? (Why?)

- Some people prefer to stay at home and not go away on holiday. What do you think? (Why?)

- In some places there are a lot of tourists. Is this a good thing for people who live there? (Why? / Why not?)

- If you could go on holiday anywhere in the world, where would you choose? (Why?)

Thank you. That is the end of the test.

> **What do you think?**
> **Do you agree?**
> **And you?**

For questions **1–8**, read the text below and decide which answer (**A**, **B**, **C** or **D**) best fits each gap. There is an example at the beginning (**0**).

Mark your answers **on the separate answer sheet**.

Example:

0   **A**   recent   **B**   current   **C**   latest   **D**   present

0	A	B	C	D
	▬	▭	▭	▭

A very unusual house

As part of an architectural project in 2010 in which people constructed egg-shaped, movable homes, Dai Haifei who was a (**0**) .... graduate, decided to build his own portable house in Beijing. (**1**) .... for his house to be environmentally-friendly, Haifei (**2**) .... use of sustainable materials, including a bamboo frame and a grass-seeded covering. The tiny house also used a solar panel for its energy (**3**) .... to a handful of electrical gadgets, and it had wood chips for insulation.

Just two metres tall at its highest point, there was only enough space for a bed, water tank, and table. For three months Haifei (**4**) .... in the 'egg house', which had no bathroom or kitchen to cook in. He (**5**) .... ate out and showered at the local pool where he paid for an annual membership.

Although Haifei only stayed in his egg house for a short period of time, he (**6**) .... the experience. He (**7**) .... that rather than it being a serious project, he had 'just wanted to play,' demonstrating his positive attitude (**8**) .... life!

1	**A** Keen	**B** Glad	**C** True	**D** Interested
2	**A** took	**B** made	**C** got	**D** did
3	**A** stock	**B** bank	**C** store	**D** supply
4	**A** occupied	**B** lived	**C** used	**D** visited
5	**A** beyond	**B** furthermore	**C** also	**D** besides
6	**A** delighted	**B** thrilled	**C** pleased	**D** enjoyed
7	**A** challenged	**B** argued	**C** presented	**D** defended
8	**A** towards	**B** over	**C** by	**D** around

For questions **9–16**, read the text below and think of the word which best fits each gap. Use only one word in each gap. There is an example at the beginning (**0**).

Write your answers **IN CAPITAL LETTERS on the answer sheet.**

Example: | **0** | A | S | | | | | | | | | | | | | | | | | |

The world's smallest frogs

Indian scientists have discovered seven new species of the tiny creatures known (**0**) .... night frogs. Some of these are (**9**) .... small that they can easily fit onto a coin or fingernail. Indeed, the smallest of the new species is just 12 millimetres long, only a little bigger than the world's smallest identified frog (**10**) .... measures an incredibly tiny 7.7 millimetres.

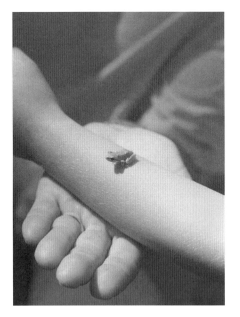

Many of the previously-identified 28 species of night frog have only been discovered in the last few years because locating them (**11**) .... be very difficult. (**12**) .... is not only because of their size, (**13**) .... because they hide away under leaves and other vegetation. They also make calls which sound (**14**) .... insects' calls and when scientists draw near, they stop calling altogether.

At the moment, the frogs are fairly widespread in certain regions of India, but they will soon need protecting due (**15**) .... an increased human presence near their habitats. Whole populations of the frogs could quickly become extinct (**16**) .... these habitats were to suddenly change.

For questions **17–24**, read the text below. Use the word given in capitals at the end of some of the lines to form a word that fits in the gap **in the same line**. There is an example at the beginning (**0**).

Write your answers **IN CAPITAL LETTERS on the separate answer sheet**.

Example: | **0** | A | V | A | I | L | A | B | I | L | I | T | Y | | | | | | |

The future of food

With the world population rising and **(0)** .... of food sources decreasing,   **AVAILABLE**
what will we be eating in the future? Food science **(17)** .... say that by   **SPECIAL**
2050, we will be consuming less meat and more fish. And with food prices rising,
another likely result is that more of us will reach the **(18)** .... that becoming   **CONCLUDE**
vegetarian is a good idea. Then there is the **(19)** .... that we will eat   **POSSIBLE**
more seaweed and insects, and perhaps even 'superfood' bars, which would be
similar to the kinds of things astronauts eat in space.

Today's technology could **(20)** .... manufacturers to produce what may   **ABLE**
become known as 'functional' foods. These are foods that are **(21)** ....   **INDIVIDUAL**
designed for different sectors of **(22)** .... This means that there will be   **SOCIAL**
foods adapted not only for babies, which we already see in supermarkets, but for teens,
women, men and elderly people, too. Because the food will be **(23)** ....   **SCIENCE**
engineered, we will also be **(24)** .... !   **HEALTH**

For questions **25–30**, complete the second sentence so that it has a similar meaning to the first sentence, using the word given. **Do not change the word given.** You must use between **two** and **five** words, including the word given. Here is an example (**0**).

Example:

0   I haven't seen you for ages!

TIME

It has .... I saw you!

The gap can be filled by the words 'been a long time since', so you write:

Example: | **0** | BEEN A LONG TIME SINCE |

Write only the missing words **IN CAPITAL LETTERS on the separate answer sheet**.

---

25   Without all your help, I wouldn't have been able to skate.
HELPED
I wouldn't have been able to skate if .... so much.

26   People say it is hard to say goodbye.
THAT
It is .... is hard.

27   They are going to deliver my new bike tomorrow.
BE
My new bike .... tomorrow.

28   Jen always misses the bus – I'm sure she has again today, too.
HAVE
Jen .... the bus again today – she always does!

29   Joseph admitted kicking the football through the window.
WHO
'It was .... the ball through the window,' said Joseph.

30   'You should come swimming with me after school,' Tracy said to me.
TO
Tracy said that .... swimming with her after school.

You are going to read a text about a survival adventure trip for young people in the mountains. For questions **31–36**, choose the answer (**A, B, C** or **D**) which you think fits best according to the text.

Mark your answers **on the separate answer sheet**.

Survival adventure camp

Last summer, I took part in a survival adventure camp in the mountains. It was run by *Survive!* Adventure Club, and the idea behind it was to give teenagers like me a taste of what it's like to survive in the wild. There were no luxuries such as showers or shops which you find on other adventure camps. That might have bothered some people – not me, though. Our guides were experienced and reassured us they'd be with us every step of the way. They provided tips to help us make informed decisions about things like where to camp, how to make meals from food we'd find ourselves, and how to get around without maps.

The experience began at the *Survive!* Adventure Club headquarters at the base of the mountains. There, we were divided into teams for the camp. The teams weren't based on age and experience but on our performance in a number of team-building tasks, which was a way for the leaders to put us together based on individual skills and personalities, to ensure a good mix in each team. We were led through a series of fun activities, such as making a raft which floated on water and taking part in a quiz. The activities were aimed at helping us make the most of our strengths, in addition to building confidence before the real survival adventure began.

Once we'd decided that we still wanted to take part after the day's activities, our first night was spent in the cabins at the club's headquarters. We had a proper bed for the night but the evening meal was down to us – I knew there'd be some kind of challenge for us! Our survival expert, Hans, gave us a lesson on finding food, such as plants, in the wild. He warned us that not everything that looks good is safe to eat, and explained that it's vital to identify what you're looking at. Hans not only pointed out what was edible or should be left alone, but also taught us to build a campfire and provided cooking tips. He told us we should use our imaginations, as cooking in the wild was different to cooking at home.

Next morning the real survival adventure began. We'd been advised to take well-fitting hiking boots, warm clothing and waterproofs. I appreciated the advice because as we soon found out, the weather in mountainous regions can be highly unpredictable. After an initial steep climb, we spent the rest of the morning identifying wildlife and learning to navigate using nature alone. We learned to determine where we were heading and what time it was. We put our cooking skills to the test at lunchtime, which was trickier than we'd imagined, though we eventually came up with something we could all eat! When evening fell, we had to locate a spot to put up our tents in. Although we'd been told there was nothing dangerous in the nearby forest, we still kept away from the edges, which put us at ease.

Over the next two days, we made a shelter, learned to treat minor injuries and built a bridge. I was put in charge of the latter and although I hadn't done anything like it previously and wasn't particularly keen to be given the responsibility, I discovered a new skill in engineering, which I never thought I'd be good at. The tasks were all fascinating and I'd like to do more of that kind of thing.

It was a wonderful adventure. I had no idea what to expect when I signed up and I wasn't an outdoors kind of person, so why I thought it was a good idea, I'm not sure! I don't regret it, though and I'm pleased I didn't quit, even when things got tougher than I ever thought they would. I always knew I was in the capable hands of the leaders and we had such good fun. I hope to be back again at some point in the future!

31 What is the writer doing in the first paragraph?

    A describing the kinds of accommodation available on the trip
    B explaining why she had some concerns about going on the trip
    C highlighting that the adventure camp she went on was unlike others
    D offering advice to other teenagers about how to cope with conditions on the trip

32 The writer says that the team-building tasks were carried out in order to

    A enable participants to get to know each other.
    B ensure each group was balanced in terms of ability.
    C provide some fun before the challenges of the trip started.
    D select those who would take part in the actual survival adventure.

33 What does the writer suggest about the first night's activity?

    A It didn't require too much creativity on the part of participants.
    B It helped participants decide whether they wanted to carry on.
    C It equipped participants with some useful knowledge.
    D It wasn't as relaxing as she had expected it to be.

34 How does the writer say she felt when the survival adventure started?

    A proud that she quickly acquired knowledge about getting around
    B grateful that she had the appropriate gear with her
    C nervous about the location she chose to camp in
    D disappointed in her cooking skills

35 What does the writer say about the activities they did on the following two days?

    A She found she was good at something she hadn't tried before.
    B She didn't enjoy some of them as much as she had hoped to.
    C She liked being put in a position of leadership for one activity.
    D She felt that experience of doing similar activities helped her.

36 How does the writer feel about having taken part in the survival adventure?

    A excited about returning as soon as she can
    B sorry that she hadn't thought of doing it before
    C surprised by how much she learned from the leaders
    D proud of herself for dealing with unexpected difficulties

You are going to read a magazine article about giving advice. Six sentences have been removed from the article. Choose from the sentences **A–G** the one which fits each gap (**37–42**). There is one extra sentence which you do not need to use.

Mark your answers **on the separate answer sheet**.

Giving advice

Journalist Nicola Hargreaves discusses whether it's worth giving advice, and if so, how?

'What do *you* think I should do?' asks your friend, as she sits down on your bed, eagerly awaiting your advice. This is no easy situation. Say something your friend disagrees with and you might feel you've disappointed her. Tell her what to do and you risk your friend feeling let down if things don't turn out as you hoped.

It's human nature to want to offer solutions when someone comes to you with a problem. It's also easy to fall into the trap of giving advice which you wouldn't take yourself, or simply reassure your friend that 'everything will be OK.' This is not particularly useful for your friend, and may leave you feeling a bit helpless, too. **37** [ ] This is because we're pleased that our friend has come to us for help, even if we don't really think we're qualified to give it. So, is it a good idea to try to give advice at all? The answer is yes... if it's done in the right way.

In fact, friends often really only want someone to listen to them. It's important, therefore, to try to work out whether they're actually seeking advice, or simply wanting to talk over whatever it is that's going round and round in their head. Doing this can, in fact, make people feel better all by themselves. There's no harm in asking whether they'd like you to suggest a solution or two, even so. **38** [ ]

It's also important to be honest. **39** [ ] Your friend won't be offended, and you can still listen carefully

and try to put yourself in their shoes. Then you can go away and think about things. What might you do if you were to experience the same thing? You can go back to your friend later with a few suggestions if you think of something that might be helpful.

40 [ ] There's nothing worse than hearing 'What *I* would have said is ...' or 'What you *should* have tried to do is ...' What's done is done and the only thing to do now is look ahead. Judging never helps anyone! If your friend keeps saying 'If only I'd ...', bring them back to the present and encourage them to think about what they can do to sort things out.

Sometimes a problem doesn't go away overnight. **41** [ ] They will definitely appreciate it if you just allow them to 'talk it out', though. Maybe they're building up courage to take action, and need to convince themselves they're doing the right thing. Just being there for them whenever they need you may be all you have to do to make things better.

Remember that you don't have to have all the answers, and your friend probably doesn't expect you to. If you're stuck, try reminding your friend of all the great things that are happening in their lives. **42** [ ] We often resolve problems when we're engaged in other activities and not directly thinking about them at all!

A If you're unable to think of a way to resolve the situation your friend finds themselves in, just say so.

B Why not plan some fun things to do together to help them forget what's going on for a while?

C Often we say this kind of thing because we believe we ought to say *something*.

D This is the first thing many of us do when we have a problem ourselves.

E Then it's up to them to say that they want to hear your ideas (or not, as the case may be).

F Can you remember a time when you weren't sure what to do, or thought you'd acted in the wrong way?

G It can be hard to listen to your friend going over and over the same thing without being able to help them.

You are going to read an article where four students talk about their dream jobs. For questions **43–52**, choose from the people (**A–D**). The people may be chosen more than once.

Mark your answers **on the separate answer sheet**.

Which student

has done a lot of research into something closely connected to a job?	43
wants to do the same thing that someone she is close to does?	44
does not know how to get into her chosen profession?	45
understands that she is unlikely to be widely recognised for work she might do?	46
likes expressing her feelings through what she does?	47
enjoys researching details related to the job?	48
hopes to encourage others to take an interest in her subject?	49
became interested in a subject when she was taught about it?	50
enjoys sharing her knowledge of a subject with other people?	51
says the reason she would like to do a job is not what people might expect?	52

Dream jobs

We asked four young people what their dream job would be and why. Here are their answers.

A Ava

'A pilot. That would be my absolute dream job. It isn't because I want to see the world, which everyone immediately thinks when I say what I want to do, though it would be a bonus if I got to spend time on the ground somewhere exotic. I don't think that happens much in reality, though. I don't even like flying that much when I'm stuck in a passenger seat staring out of a tiny window at the clouds. I'd rather be up front taking charge! One of my hobbies is making model aeroplanes with my dad. I know they can't fly, and I know they're nothing like the real thing, but every time we bring a new one home to build, I go online and look up everything I can about it. I've not only built hundreds of models but I've built up my knowledge about planes, too. I'm also really into physics at school and I just think flying is really interesting.'

B Emily

'I've had hearing difficulties since I was really young, and I often just zone out and stop trying to keep up with things when there's a lot of background noise – it can be tricky trying to keep up with my friends' conversations. My parents are both deaf, so I've been able to use sign language for as long as I can remember. I'm teaching my friends now, so we can communicate more easily if we're somewhere noisy. They love it and I've discovered how much I love teaching them. We have a laugh when one of them gets it wrong and signs something funny by mistake. So my aim is to be a sign language teacher. I'm unsure about how to go about it yet and it's still a pretty new idea but I'm determined to find out what I can about it and make sure I get the right qualifications.'

C Sophia

'I want to be a poet. I've been writing my own poems for a couple of years. The kind of stuff I do is called 'slam' poetry. It's where you reflect on life experiences. It's emotional and passionate and comes straight from the heart. I got interested in it when a poet came to school and gave us a workshop on it. He taught us about how to make the words flow and how to say it aloud. Slam poetry's performed in competitions and I've won two now. I was so nervous the first time I stood up but then I focussed on the message I wanted to get across to the audience and then it just seemed easy. I'd love to get my poems published and carry on giving performances. People overlook poetry a bit but this is the kind of style that gets noticed!'

D Mia

'My mum's a research scientist and I hope to follow in her footsteps. I'm pretty good at science at school and I love biology. I think I'd like to work on developing medicines. That's something that can really change the world, make a big difference to people's lives. I'm fairly realistic about it, though. I know I'll have to do years of study and groundwork before I get to any of the really exciting stuff. Even then, I'm probably not going to be a world-famous scientist, like Einstein. I know I'll just be a tiny part of the whole process but I still think it would be amazing to work on the next big discovery, the next big cure. Imagine that! I also want to get more girls into science. A lot of the girls in my class want to be actors or singers but that's not very practical, is it?'

You **must** answer this question. Write your answer in **140–190** words in an appropriate style **on the separate answer sheet**.

1   In your English class you have been talking about shopping. Now your English teacher has asked you to write an essay for homework.

Write your essay using **all** the notes and giving reasons for your point of view.

'Shops are no longer necessary because people can buy
everything they want on the internet.'

Do you agree?

Notes

Write about:

1. the time it takes to buy things

2. how easy it is to choose what to buy

3. .... (your own idea)

Write an answer to **one** of the questions **2–5** in this part. Write your answer in **140–190** words in an appropriate style **on the separate answer sheet**. Put the question number in the box at the top of the answer sheet.

2   You see this announcement in an English-language magazine for teenagers.

Articles wanted   **Photographs**

Why do people take so many photographs? Are photographs the best way of remembering people and events? What do you take photographs of and why?

Tell us what you think. The best article will win a prize!

Write your **article**.

3   Your English teacher has asked you to write a story for the school magazine.

Your story must begin with this sentence:

Harry looked up when he heard the noise and smiled.

Your story must include:

• a visitor

• a present

Write your **story**.

4   You have received this email from your English-speaking friend, Sam.

Hi!

I live quite near my school and want to walk there every day with my friends. My mum says I have to go in the car with her instead. I get on well with my mum and don't want her to be upset, but I don't want her to take me to school anymore. What should I do?

Write your **email**.

5   Answer the following question based on the set text.

In your English class, you have been discussing the characters in the set text. Now your teacher wants you to write an essay answering the following question:

'The book would be better if the writer had included and described more characters.' Do you agree?

Write your **essay**.

🎧 35 You will hear people talking in eight different situations. For questions **1–8**, choose the best answer (**A**, **B** or **C**).

1   You hear two friends talking about going to a new chess club at their school.
    They both hope that playing chess will

    A   encourage them to reduce their screen time.
    B   improve their problem-solving skills.
    C   help to increase their self-confidence.

2   You hear a teacher telling her class about a shelter they are going to build in the woods.
    What is she doing?

    A   warning them not to make their design too sophisticated
    B   advising them of the best way to approach the task
    C   encouraging them to be as creative as possible

3   You hear a boy talking to a friend about seeing his painting displayed in a competition.
    How does he feel about the competition now?

    A   concerned that the message he tried to put across is too difficult
    B   astonished at the level of entries he's competing against
    C   confident that his work is up to the standard of other entrants

4   You hear a student telling his class about a special boat race he took part in.
    What does he think contributed to his team's success?

    A   the level of their knowledge of engineering
    B   a chance event near the end of their race
    C   their determination to row as hard as possible

5   You hear a girl phoning her father.
    Why is she phoning him?

    A   to ask him to do her a favour
    B   to remind him about what they'd agreed
    C   to give him more information about a plan

6   You hear two friends talking about a summer reading project they're involved in.
    What does the girl say about her progress?

    A   She is further behind schedule than their classmates.
    B   She has struggled to find a book that she's really enjoyed.
    C   She has had too many recommendations to get through.

7   You hear a teacher talking about a tour of a film studio she has organised for her class.
    What does she think the students will gain from the trip?

    A   a better understanding of the director's influence on the film
    B   a unique insight into where one particular film was made
    C   more appreciation for what happens behind the scenes in a film

8   You hear a boy telling a friend about a book he's reading.
    How does the book compare with his expectations?

    A   The subject matter is more serious.
    B   The quality of the images is better.
    C   The storyline is more complex.

36 You will hear a girl called Katie giving a class presentation about a bat-watching trip she went on recently. For questions **9–18**, complete the sentences with a word or short phrase.

Bat-watching trip

Katie and her dad were joined on their trip by a family friend, whose job involves
(9) ....

Katie describes the boat they went on as not feeling **(10)** .... initially.

Their guide said that one reason bats are important is for helping to spread **(11)** ....

Katie learnt that a shortage of insects can quickly cause **(12)** .... in bats out hunting.

Katie used a machine called a **(13)** .... to hear the sounds the bats made.

Katie compares the sounds of bats calling to a strange kind of **(14)** ....

Katie was grateful for the **(15)** .... that had been supplied for the trip.

A number of bats appeared on part of the river with a long **(16)** .... on the bank.

Their friend managed to spot some **(17)** .... above them during their trip.

Katie was pleased that the money from their tickets was going to a **(18)** ....

37 You will hear five teenage writers talking about listening to music while studying. For questions **19–23**, choose from the list (**A–H**) the advice each speaker gives. Use the letters only once. There are three extra letters which you do not need to use.

A   It depends on the kind of studying I'm doing.

B   It only works well with certain types of music.

Speaker 1 ⬜ **19**

C   I've had to accept it doesn't work for me.

Speaker 2 ⬜ **20**

D   It makes even boring subjects more appealing.

Speaker 3 ⬜ **21**

E   I do it when I really want to concentrate.

Speaker 4 ⬜ **22**

F   It's helped me to remember certain things.

G   It's easier for me than studying in complete silence.

Speaker 5 ⬜ **23**

H   It's only really useful during study breaks.

38 You will hear an interview with a student called Ella about the work experience she is currently doing as a lighting technician. For questions **24–30**, choose the best answer (**A**, **B** or **C**).

24   Ella suggests that her interest in lighting started with

    A   the lights she once saw at a theatre show.
    B   an outstanding light show at a rock concert.
    C   the effects of a fireworks display.

25   Ella says that the work of theatre lighting technicians

    A   can vary according to the director they're working with.
    B   can be more complex than she'd initially realised.
    C   can be important for people's understanding of a play.

26   Ella thinks that members of a theatre audience

    A   only really notice the lighting when something goes wrong.
    B   generally appreciate what good lighting adds to a performance.
    C   rarely react to lighting effects.

27   Ella mentions an early lighting plan she made at school that

    A   relied on technology that the school didn't have.
    B   was too difficult for anyone to follow.
    C   overlooked a key point about the play it was intended for.

28   During her research into theatre lighting, Ella

    A   felt disappointed to find that she knew so little about it.
    B   was impressed at what theatres achieved before using electricity.
    C   wondered whether modern lighting has spoilt the atmosphere in theatres.

29   After seeing the technology available for modern theatre lighting, Ella

    A   is excited by the creative possibilities it offers.
    B   thinks it has made a technician's job easier than it used to be.
    C   has realised it's important not to use it unnecessarily.

30   What does Ella feel might be a disadvantage of the job?

    A   It will probably always involve long hours.
    B   She may never become famous for what she does.
    C   It could take her years to reach the top of her profession.

Part 1   2 minutes [3 minutes for groups of three]

Interlocutor First we'd like to know something about you.

Future plans

- What are you going to do next weekend? (Why?)
- What plans do you have for next year? (Why?)
- What would you like to do when you leave school? (Why?)
- Do you think you might live and work in another country in the future? (Why? / Why not?)

Part 2   4 minutes [6 minutes for groups of three]

Interlocutor In this part of the test, I'm going to give each of you two photographs. I'd like you to talk about your photographs on your own for about a minute, and also to answer a question about your partner's photographs.

(*Candidate A*), it's your turn first. Here are your photographs on page C15 of the Speaking appendix. They show **people studying in different places**.

I'd like you to compare the photographs, and say **why you think the people have decided to study in these places**.

All right?

Candidate A
🕐 *1 minute* ....

Interlocutor Thank you.

(*Candidate B*), **do you enjoy studying outside? (Why? / Why not?)**

Candidate B
🕐 *Approximately 30 seconds* ....

Interlocutor Thank you.

Now (*Candidate B*), here are your photographs on page C16 of the Speaking appendix. They show **people travelling in cities in different ways**.

I'd like you to compare the photographs, and say **why you think the people have chosen to travel in the city in these ways**.

All right?

Candidate B
🕐 *1 minute* ....

Interlocutor Thank you.

(*Candidate A*), **which of these ways would you prefer to travel in a city? (Why?)**

Candidate A
🕐 *Approximately 30 seconds* ....

Interlocutor Thank you.

Interlocutor Now I'd like you to talk about something together for about two minutes.

I'd like you to imagine that a school wants to encourage students to use their free time well and has asked for ideas of activities. Here are some ideas and a question for you to discuss.

First you have some time to look at the task on page C17 of the Speaking appendix.

Now talk to each other about **whether these are useful ways for young people to spend their free time**.

Candidates

🕐 *2 minutes (3 minutes for groups of three)*

Interlocutor Thank you. Now you have about a minute to decide **which is the least useful way for young people to spend their free time**.

Candidates

🕐 *1 minute (for pairs and groups of three)*

Interlocutor Thank you.

| Part 4 | 4 minutes [6 minutes for groups of three] |

Interlocutor

- Do you think young people have enough free time nowadays or too much? (Why?)

- Some people say the school day is too long. What do you think? (Why?)

- Do you think young people get enough sleep? (Why? / Why not?)

- Some people say everyone is too busy to enjoy free time nowadays. Do you agree? (Why? / Why not?)

- Is it better to watch sport or take part in it? (Why?)

- Do you think everyone should carry on learning new things even after they've left school? (Why? / Why not?)

| What do you think? |
| Do you agree? |
| And you? |

Thank you. That is the end of the test.

For questions **1–8**, read the text below and decide which answer (**A**, **B**, **C** or **D**) best fits each gap. There is an example at the beginning (**0**).

Mark your answers **on the separate answer sheet**.

Example:

0   **A**   established   **B**   located   **C**   placed   **D**   positioned

```
0 │ A    B    C    D
  │ ▭    ▬    ▭    ▭
```

The world's quietest railway station

Some of the world's most heavily used railway stations are **(0)** .... in Japan. According to **(1)**..................., 45 out of the 51 busiest in the world are in the country. Some 3.6 million passengers travel through the busiest railway station, Shinjuku Station in Tokyo, every **(2)** .... day.

But surprisingly, this small but **(3)** .... populated country also has some stations which are hardly used at all. Kyu-Shirataki Station, on the island of Hokkaido is in such a **(4)** .... place that it was only used by one person for a few years. High school student Kana Harada was a **(5)** .... passenger before it closed in 2016. The train stopped every morning to take high school student Kana Harada to school, and every afternoon to drop her back at Kyu-Shirataki.

But keeping the station open for just one passenger was simply not **(6)** .... Therefore the operator of the line, Hokkaido Railway Company, planned to close the station **(7)** .... But when they found out that this would leave Kana with no **(8)** ...., they agreed to keep the line open until she graduated from school. Although trains still use the line, the station itself is now completely abandoned.

1   **A** measurements   **B** numbers   **C** sizes   **D** statistics

2   **A** individual   **B** one   **C** particular   **D** single

3   **A** considerably   **B** densely   **C** largely   **D** mainly

4   **A** far   **B** homeless   **C** remote   **D** separated

5   **A** common   **B** regular   **C** usual   **D** typical

6   **A** commercial   **B** profitable   **C** successful   **D** valuable

7   **A** always   **B** constantly   **C** lastly   **D** permanently

8   **A** transport   **B** journey   **C** travel   **D** vehicle

For questions **9–16**, read the text below and think of the word which best fits the gap. Use only **one** word in each gap. There is an example at the beginning (**0**).

Write your answer **IN CAPITAL LETTERS on the separate answer sheet**.

Example:
| 0 | | O | N | | | | | | | | | | | | | | | | |

A possible solution to a major health problem

by Andrew Kerr, Health Correspondent

New research shows that an unhealthy diet can actually have a damaging effect **(0)** .... the brains and the behaviour of secondary school pupils. Some teenagers virtually live on junk food, **(9)**..................... instance burgers and chocolate. These are often widely available, and can **(10)** .... bought on the way to or from school. For some teenagers, junk food makes up as **(11)** .... as 30 percent of their diet. What's more, fewer than one in ten teenagers eat the recommended five daily portions **(12)** .... fruit and vegetables. Experts are warning of a nutrition crisis in **(13)** .... teenagers are deprived of essential dairy products and proteins.

But **(14)** .... to new research by Oxford University, giving teenagers a health supplement pill can really help. The vast majority of teenagers in the UK eat absolutely **(15)** .... fish at all, and the pill contains fish oil that is essential for the teenage brain. Researchers found that this led to a reduction **(16)** .... poor concentration and improved academic performance.

For questions **17–24**, read the text below. Use the word given in capitals at the end of some of the lines to form a word that fits in the gap **in the same line**. There is an example at the beginning (**0**).

Write your answer **IN CAPITAL LETTERS on the separate answer sheet**.

Example: | 0 | | P | O | W | E | R | F | U | L | | | | | | | | | | |

Hope in a Ballet Shoe – a dancer's life story

Hope in a Ballet Shoe is the **(0)** .... autobiography of ballet **POWER**
dancer Michaela DePrince.

Michaela had a strict **(17)** .... in Sierra Leone. There are several **BRING**
(18) .... of her early days there which are particularly well-written. **DESCRIBE**
A turning point in her life was her **(19)** .... by an American couple **ADOPT**
at the age of four, and her move with them to the USA. At first, she found that
all the cultural **(20)** .... were hard to get used to. But she grew to **DIFFERENT**
love her new home, and the book shows how love and **(21)** .... **PATIENT**
can overcome these difficulties – and help people to achieve their goals.
Michaela was absolutely **(22)** .... to become a ballet dancer **DETERMINE**
and practised for hours on end. Her family were there for her all the time,
supporting her and eventually **(23)** .... her to succeed. Michaela **ABLE**
is now a world-famous ballerina with the Dutch National Ballet.

I would certainly recommend *Hope in a Ballet Shoe* to anyone from the age of
eleven upwards. It truly is a **(24)** .... story. **MOVE**

For questions **25–30**, complete the second sentence so that it has a similar meaning to the first sentence, using the word given. **Do not change the word given.** You must use between **two** and **five** words, including the word given. Here is an example (**0**).

Example:

0   I haven't seen you for ages!

     TIME

     It has .... I saw you!

The gap can be filled by the words 'been a long time since', so you write:

Example: | **0** | BEEN A LONG TIME SINCE |

Write only the missing words **IN CAPITAL LETTERS on the separate answer sheet**.

---

25   Tina's grandparents raised her.
     BROUGHT
     Tina .... her grandparents.

26   I'm surprised she declined my invitation to the party.
     CAN'T
     I .... down my invitation to the party.

27   When John told me what had happened, I believed him.
     WORD
     When John told me what had happened, I .... it.

28   I often cycle by myself at the weekend.
     FOR
     I often go .... my own at the weekend.

29   She only bought the book because the teacher said it was good.
     HAVE
     She wouldn't .... the teacher hadn't said it was good.

30   I want someone to cut my hair.
     GET
     I'd .... cut.

You are going to read a magazine article about a new type of hotel. For questions **31–36**, choose the answer (**A**, **B**, **C** or **D**) which you think fits best according to the text.

Mark your answers **on the separate answer sheet**.

Hotels of the future

Our travel correspondent Joanna Richards reports about a new trend in hotels.

I recently visited a hotel in France which has no visible human staff. This is just one of several hotels in Europe and Asia which runs with apparently no human contact. Most of the services are provided by robots and machines. The concept is to provide an environmentally friendly hotel where staff and running costs are kept to a minimum. Personally, I've spent my life away from robots and machines, and so kept having to remind myself that in many parts of the world, its not unusual for jobs and household tasks to be automated these days.

So I lost no time in booking myself a room at one of these hotels and going to see it for myself. And sure enough, there at the reception desk instead of a friendly receptionist wearing a uniform was a machine.

'I'd like to check in please, I shouted, wondering if the machine would respond to my voice, and feeling thrilled that I was about to have my first ever conversation with a check-in machine. Nothing. I said it again but there was silence. I was hoping the machine would say something like 'If you want to check in, press 1. But then I noticed a written message in the machine's screen. 'Please insert your credit card and key in your booking reference, then follow the instructions.' No conversation. How disappointing.

line 23

Staying at the hotel costs from €35 (more if you want a bigger room). That's a bargain for Paris, where a stay in a more conventional hotel can easily cost two or three times that much. And if you did stay there, it wouldn't necessarily be any nicer, and certainly wouldn't be any more memorable. The hotel is located near to the amusement park, Disneyland Paris, which was created as a visitor attraction on the east of the city with lots of amusement rides. In fact, many of the guests book the hotel purely in order to be close to the park.

Back in the hotel, as well as machines to check in, there are vending machines to serve drinks and snacks and vacuum cleaners that work without a human, using sensors to navigate around the rooms. According to the owners, the laundry has robots which do all the washing unaided. Another innovation is the use of face recognition instead of keys to get into your room. A photograph of the guest's face is taken at the reception desk by the check in machines.

With 60 rooms in the building, there is a lot of coming and going. Guests are actively encouraged to stop and get a coffee from one of the machines in the guest lounge with other guests, so there is at least some social interaction. One area where humans are absolutely essential for the hotel is security. There are scanners and CCTV cameras everywhere, and the footage from these is watched by human security guards, no matter whether or not the hotel is full. It is their job to make sure that the guests are safe – and that no-one causes any damage to hotel property, including of course making off with a costly robot.

Critics say that businesses like these automated hotels will mean that people lose their jobs, as more and more roles can be performed by robots and machines. But there are many who see them as a vision of the future and argue that robots can make our lives easier. But this can only happen if higher manufacturing and operating standards are achieved, and if guests are prepared to put their trust in machines and don't mind the lack of personal contact. Only then will this type of hotel be a success. Time will tell if this is the case.

line 62

31 The aim of this hotel is to be very

    A   efficient.
    B   friendly.
    C   profitable.
    D   unusual.

32 What aspect of the writer's experience at reception was 'disappointing' (line 23)?

    A   the appearance of the reception
    B   the time she wasted checking in
    C   the lack of verbal interaction with the machine
    D   the rudeness of the other guests

33 What does the writer say about the price of the rooms in the hotel?

    A   The hotel is good value.
    B   The prices are likely to rise.
    C   Other hotels provide better accommodation.
    D   It is not always clear how much a room will cost.

34 What is the writer's main point in the fifth paragraph?

    A   There are limits to what robots and machines can do.
    B   Robots and machines can learn a wide range of skills.
    C   Different robots and machines are used for different tasks.
    D   Humans make mistakes that robots and machines do not make.

35 What risk is mentioned in the sixth paragraph?

    A   robots being stolen
    B   security guards being ineffective
    C   the hotel not doing enough business
    D   areas of the hotel becoming too crowded

36 What does 'this can only happen' in line 62 refer to?

    A   more roles being performed by robots and machines
    B   many seeing the hotel as a vision of the future
    C   robots and machines making our lives easier
    D   reduction in social human contact

You are going to read an article about a young mountaineer called George Atkinson. Six sentences have been removed from the article. Choose from the sentences **A–G** the one which fits each gap (**37–42**). There is one extra sentence which you do not need to use.

Mark your answers **on the separate answer sheet**.

Making mountaineering history

At the beginning of April, just a few weeks before his 17th birthday, George Atkinson arrived in Kathmandu in Nepal. The schoolboy from London was about to begin the final stage of his quest to become the youngest person to climb the highest peak on each of the world's seven continents. **37** [ ] It was just Mount Everest to go – the mightiest of the lot.

As an 11-year-old, George had been with his father on an organised trip up Mount Kilimanjaro, Africa's highest mountain. But George's dad got a stomach bug before the final ascent to the peak. 'I felt very weak and dehydrated', he said, and had to go back down. **38** [ ] And as George continued to the top with the rest of the group, his father endured an anxious wait. 'Seeing him coming back down again was indescribable.'

The next few years saw George build up his mountaineering skills and his fitness to prepare for his epic challenge. He spent his weekends carrying a heavily laden 80-litre backpack and walking from the family home to Richmond Park in London, which he'd then complete two full circuits of, making a round trip of 30 kilometres.

At 29,029 feet, Everest is over 6,500 feet higher than any of the other mountains on George's list. He knew it would be a challenge and was aware of the risks that being at such high altitudes carries, but he wanted to stand on top of the world. On checking in to the Hotel Everest View, at 12,729 feet, he got a glimpse of Mount Everest, and imagined looking back down to the hotel from the peak. He phoned his mother, Penny, and spoke to her. **39** [ ] And she knew just how much this climb meant to him.

But as they got closer to the summit, the weather turned bad. There were nervous moments for George and his group as they waited to see if the weather would improve and the wind would drop to a safer speed of below 30 miles an hour. George didn't know how long he might have to wait for another opportunity. **40** [ ] An American climber, Jordan Romero, who was two months younger than George, only needed to scale Vinson Massif in Antarctica to complete his set of seven.

But eventually they made it, and George achieved his dream. But there was hardly time to celebrate on the peak. **41** [ ] By the time they got back down to the bottom, George and the rest of his group were all exhausted.

George intends to keep climbing and carry on with his studies. He says he is looking forward to life getting back to normal. And he's planning another mountaineering trip with his dad, this time up Mont Blanc in France. But the question is, will the elder Atkinson make it all the way up to the top this time? **42** [ ]

A	'I've seen it,' he said, 'and it's huge.'		**E**	But George knew what he wanted: he was going to carry on.
B	He had already conquered all but one.			
			F	And by then, someone else might have snatched the record.
C	But he knew he still needed more practice.			
D	'I hope so,' he says, 'George is going to carry my stuff.'		**G**	Almost immediately, they had to begin an exhausting, non-stop 20-hour descent.

You are going to read four reviews of autobiographies in which the writers described their lives as teenagers. For questions **43–52**, choose from the writers (**A–D**). The writers may be chosen more than once.

Which writer

knew at an early age what career he would choose? | 43 |

did not enjoy his education? | 44 |

was not brought up by his parents? | 45 |

was very critical of one person? | 46 |

invented some details in his book? | 47 |

worked on the book with another author? | 48 |

described other people very well? | 49 |

told of the good and bad times of his early career? | 50 |

was confused about what he had to learn? | 51 |

described how the place where he lived changed over time? | 52 |

Reviews of famous autobiographers who wrote about being teenagers

A   Winston Churchill – politician

Churchill wrote the first volume of his autobiography in 1930, nine years before becoming Prime Minister of the UK. Called *My Early Life*, it covered the time from his birth in 1870, when he grew up in a very grand house as the neglected son of a wealthy aristocratic who were too busy to spend much time with him. Instead, he spent his days – and developed his strongest bond – with the nanny who looked after him. Although he went on to become an excellent writer and perhaps the outstanding European politician of his day, the boy Churchill detested being made to study, and wrote entertainingly about his schoolmaster's attempts to teach him Latin. When instructed that 'mensa' meant 'oh, table' and informed that this was what you would say if you were talking to a table, young Churchill did not see why he needed to know this, and replied that he couldn't see the point. 'But I never do,' he said. His teacher didn't see the funny side, which, fortunately for us, makes the book all the more entertaining.

B   Laurie Lee – poet

Laurie Lee's classic memoir *Cider With Rosie* tells of his childhood in a remote valley in England's Cotswold Hills in the early years of the twentieth century. At the start of the book, the valley seemed to have developed little in hundreds of years; by the end, a bus service and electricity have arrived; Lee's village was no longer so remote, but was now fully connected to the modern world. Much of the book shows what a remarkable woman Laurie's mother was, raising him and his brothers and sisters with little help from anyone else. As he grows older, he senses a feeling that he was born to be a poet. He was right of course, and besides his poetry, Lee also produced plays, short stories and travel books, as well as this autobiographical masterpiece, which is as alive now as the day it was written.

C   Robbie Williams – singer

The former singer of the British boy band Take That released his autobiography *You Know Me* after two decades being one of the most famous musicians on the planet. Starting with his childhood in Stoke-on-Trent, it tells of the successes and hard times Robbie experienced after becoming a superstar. *You Know Me* was clearly aimed at his fans, many of whom would probably already have bought *Feel*, the 2004 biography of Williams written by journalist Chris Heath, who also collaborated on this publication. So how is *You Know Me* different? Well, there are plenty of anecdotes, gathered from informal interviews Heath conducted with Williams, which provide insight not just into the man himself, but into the music industry as a whole.

D   Gerald Durrell – wildlife writer

British naturalist Gerald Durrell wrote this account of the years he spent aged 10 to 15 living on the island of Corfu. His eccentric family and the inhabitants of Corfu are portrayed brilliantly. Gerald's brother Lawrence in particular emerges as a bad-tempered, mean and unreasonable young man. It's tempting to think that Lawrence (who also became a writer) must have been outraged by the book's publication. But apparently he both liked it, and praised its accuracy. Although it is an autobiography, not all the 'facts' in the book are actually correct: for example, some of the family actually lived in a different part of the island, rather than all in the same home as the book claimed.

You **must** answer this question. Write your answer in **140–190** words in an appropriate style **on the separate answer sheet**.

1   In your English class you have been talking about free time. Now your English teacher has asked you to write an essay.

Write your essay using **all** the notes and giving reasons for your point of view.

Should teenagers spend their free time doing lots of activities, or is it better for teenagers to spend most of their free time relaxing?

Notes

Write about:

    1. learning new things

    2. time with friends

    3. .... (your own idea)

Write an answer to **one** of the questions **2–5** in this part. Write your answer in **140–190** words in an appropriate style **on the separate answer sheet**. Put the question number in the box at the top of the answer sheet.

2   You see this announcement on an English-language website for teenagers.

> # Reviews wanted!
>
> Tell us about a museum that you have visited. Describe the museum. What can you see there? What do you like about the museum? What didn't you like? Who would you recommend the museum to?
>
> We will post the most interesting reviews on the website.

Write your **review**.

3   This is part of a letter you receive from an English friend.

> *I'm not very fit and I'd like to take up a sport, but I don't know what sport I should do. Have you got any ideas? What else could I do to be more healthy?*

Write your **letter**.

4   Your English teacher has asked you to write a story for the class website.

Your story must begin with this sentence:

Anna was surprised to see so many people in the room.

Your story must include:
• a competition
• a happy ending

Write your **story**.

5   Answer the following question based on the set text.

You see this notice in an English-language magazine for teenagers.

> # Places in books
>
> Tell us about a place described in a book you have read. Was this place important to the story? What effect did the place have on the characters in the story?
>
> The best articles will appear on our website!

Write your **article**.

🎧39) You will hear people talking in eight different situations. For questions **1–8**, choose the best answer (**A**, **B** or **C**).

1   You hear a boy telling his class about a music workshop he attended with other students from his school.
     What does he say about the workshop?

     A   It inspired them to attempt things they hadn't tried before.
     B   It confirmed their confidence in their ability to compose.
     C   It gave them a great opportunity to work with professional musicians.

2   You hear a girl telling her friend about a long train trip she went on.
     What does she say about it?

     A   It took longer than she'd expected.
     B   It felt more uncomfortable than usual.
     C   It was too noisy for her to do her homework.

3   You hear a theatre actor giving a talk to some drama students.
     What does he emphasise about his work?

     A   the advantages of always being asked to play the same kind of character
     B   the difficulties of playing someone who is very different from him
     C   the energy required to repeat the same role over many performances

4   You hear a girl talking to her teacher about her homework.
     What is her problem?

     A   She's taken on something that's too extensive in scale.
     B   She's found it difficult to identify reliable sources of information.
     C   She's struggled to find a topic that's really inspired her.

5   You hear a girl phoning her mother about a friend she was supposed to meet.
     How does she feel now about the meeting?

     A   concerned about her friend's excuse for cancelling
     B   cross that her friend failed to contact her in advance
     C   embarrassed that she gave her friend the wrong information

6   You hear a science teacher talking to his class about an experiment they are going to do.
     What does he tell them?

     A   that the reaction they are hoping for may happen very suddenly
     B   that only following his instructions carefully can guarantee success
     C   that they should be prepared to observe minor changes

7   You hear two friends talking about a carnival that has just taken place in their town.
     What do they agree about it?

     A   It was more exciting in previous years.
     B   It had more to attract teenagers than other local events.
     C   It provided young people with a great chance to perform.

8   You hear a teacher talking to her student about a story he's written.
     What is she doing?

     A   explaining which parts particularly impressed her
     B   giving hints as to how he could develop his writing skills
     C   trying to establish where his ideas came from

🎧 40 You will hear a boy called Harry telling his class about an art event he took part in recently. For questions **9–18**, complete the sentences with a word or short phrase.

Art Day

Fiona, the person running the art day, had once worked as a **(9)** ....

Harry uses the word **(10)** .... to describe his feelings when he first arrived.

Harry was inspired by the variety of **(11)** .... paper in the drawing book he was given.

Harry put a **(12)** .... on the cover of his drawing book.

Harry's first painting was a **(13)** ....

Harry was particularly impressed by the **(14)** .... that another student had done.

With Fiona's help, Harry attempted a more **(15)** .... style of drawing than he'd tried when he started.

After lunch, the group chose the theme of the **(16)** .... for the sculpture they intended to make together.

Harry found a collection of **(17)** .... to include in the sculpture.

The **(18)** .... of the art group was what made Harry decide to sign up for the next session.

41 You will hear five teenagers talking about playing tennis. For questions **19–23**, choose from the list (**A–H**) the reason each speaker gives for enjoying the game. Use the letters only once. There are three extra letters which you do not need to use.

A   It helps me to relax.

B   I'm learning to cope with pressure.   Speaker 1 | 19 |

C   It's a great mental challenge.

                                                                    Speaker 2 | 20 |

D   I like the chance to be competitive.

                                                                    Speaker 3 | 21 |

E   It's a good way to make friends.

                                                                    Speaker 4 | 22 |

F   It's more fun than other forms of exercise.

G   It's taught me how to accept losing.   Speaker 5 | 23 |

H   I've improved a lot through working hard.

🎧 42 You will hear an interview with a girl called Lucy Hughes, who is talking about her love of maths. For questions **24–30**, choose the best answer (**A, B** or **C**).

24 What first made Lucy excited about maths?

    A   taking part in a maths activity at school
    B   being able to use the basic maths skills she'd learnt
    C   recognising a link between maths and the natural world

25 What does Lucy's dad suggest about some people attending his training sessions?

    A   They don't realise that maths is easier than they think.
    B   A lack of confidence discourages them from using maths.
    C   Having to remember so much has put them off maths.

26 How have Lucy's parents helped her with maths?

    A   by giving her practical maths problems to solve
    B   by taking her to local events connected with maths
    C   by working through difficult maths homework with her

27 Lucy suggests the appeal of maths for her is that

    A   there is a limitless number of areas to explore.
    B   there is always a single clear and definite answer.
    C   there is more than one method for working out the same solution.

28 When Lucy entered a maths competition recently, she

    A   was worried by the level of the other competitors.
    B   felt confident once it was her turn to perform.
    C   only realised close to the end that she could actually win it.

29 What did Lucy discover during the competition?

    A   that people from a range of cultures have similar attitudes to maths
    B   that people in different countries solve maths problems in the same way
    C   that people with no shared languages can understand the same maths problems

30 Lucy thinks that in the future

    A   she will need maths to study science at a high level.
    B   she wants to train to become a maths teacher.
    C   she would like to just enjoy maths purely as a hobby.

Part 1   2 minutes [3 minutes for groups of three]

Interlocutor First we'd like to know something about you.

Entertainment

- Do you prefer to watch films at home or in the cinema? (Why?)
- Tell us about a film you've really enjoyed.
- Do you prefer going out with your friends or with your family? (Why?)
- How much time do you spend online every day? (Why?)
- What kind of TV programmes or videos do you enjoy most? (Why?)

Part 2   4 minutes [6 minutes for groups of three]

Interlocutor In this part of the test, I'm going to give each of you two photographs. I'd like you to talk about your photographs on your own for about a minute, and also to answer a question about your partner's photographs.

(*Candidate A*), it's your turn first. Here are your photographs on page C18 of the Speaking appendix. They show **people playing different games**.

I'd like you to compare the photographs, and say **what you think the people are enjoying about playing these games**.

All right?

Candidate A
🕐 *1 minute* ....

Interlocutor Thank you.

(*Candidate B*), **which of these games would you prefer to play? (Why?)**

Candidate B
🕐 *Approximately 30 seconds* ....

Interlocutor Thank you.

Now (*Candidate B*), here are your photographs on page C19 of the Speaking appendix. They show **people who are concentrating on tasks in different situations**.

I'd like you to compare the photographs, and say **why you think the people need to concentrate in these situations**.

All right?

Candidate B
🕐 *1 minute* ....

Interlocutor Thank you.

(*Candidate A*), **do you find it easy to concentrate? (Why? / Why not?)**

Candidate A
🕐 *Approximately 30 seconds* ....

Interlocutor Thank you.

Part 3

Interlocutor Now I'd like you to talk about something together for about two minutes.

Here are some things which many people spend a lot of time doing every day and a question for you to discuss.

First you have some time to look at the task on page C20 of the Speaking appendix.

Now talk to each other about **whether it's important to spend a lot of time doing these things every day**.

Candidates

🕐 *2 minutes (3 minutes for groups of three)*

Interlocutor Thank you. Now you have about a minute to decide **which thing everyone should spend some time doing every day.**

Candidates

🕐 *1 minute (for pairs and groups of three)*

Interlocutor Thank you.

Part 4   4 minutes [6 minutes for groups of three]

Interlocutor

- Do you think it's a good idea to have a daily routine? (Why? / Why not?)

- Should people try to read news stories every day? (Why? / Why not?)

- Is it boring to do the same things all the time? (Why? / Why not?)

- If you want to be good at something like music, how important is it to practise regularly? (Why?)

- Do you prefer to meet friends face-to-face or communicate with them online?

- Do you think it's possible to be good friends with someone if you don't see them every day? (Why? / Why not?)

Thank you. That is the end of the test.

What do you think? Do you agree? And you?

For questions **1–8**, read the text below and decide which answer (**A, B, C** or **D**) best fits each gap. There is an example at the beginning (**0**).

Mark your answers **on the separate answer sheet**.

Example:

0   **A**   definite   **B**   specific   **C**   fixed   **D**   particular

```
0   A   B   C   D
    ▬   ▭   ▭   ▭
```

Chickens are smarter than you think

Ask people whether they think chickens are intelligent and most of them will answer a (**0**) .... 'no'. This is because we (**1**) .... to think of mammals, such as cats, dogs or horses, as being smarter than birds. We also believe that birds like chickens do not feel emotions in the same way other animals do.

Research has (**2**) .... , however, that this is not necessarily the (**3**) .... Chickens do observe each other's (**4**) .... , which means they can not only learn from each other but are able to notice how other chickens are feeling too. The research proves that chickens have minds: they have memory, thinking ability and emotions, and are (**5**) .... of others and their surroundings. Chickens also (**6**) .... that they have complex social structures, often thought to be a unique (**7**) .... of mammals. Chickens, then, are just as sensitive as we are, and it is important for us to recognise this in our (**8**) .... of them.

1	**A** regard	**B** consider	**C** tend	**D** assess
2	**A** indicated	**B** expressed	**C** advised	**D** displayed
3	**A** matter	**B** point	**C** case	**D** fact
4	**A** action	**B** behaviour	**C** manner	**D** practice
5	**A** familiar	**B** wise	**C** clear	**D** aware
6	**A** declare	**B** confirm	**C** demonstrate	**D** expose
7	**A** characteristic	**B** nature	**C** style	**D** personality
8	**A** management	**B** approach	**C** dealings	**D** treatment

For questions **9–16**, read the text below and think of the word which best fits each gap. Use only **one** word in each gap. There is an example at the beginning (**0**).

Write your answers **IN CAPITAL LETTERS on the separate answer sheet**.

Example: | 0 | | I | F | | | | | | | | | | | | | | | | |

What is futsal?

(0) .... you're into football, there's no doubt you'll like futsal, too. You may already have heard of this exciting, fast-paced sport, **(9)** .... how is it played? Recognised around the world **(10)** .... official football associations, futsal is similar to football, though it is different in significant ways. **(11)** .... than being played on a large outdoor pitch, futsal is usually played on hard indoor courts, **(12)** .... much smaller goals than football and never more than five players. The ball is smaller and less bouncy than an ordinary football. Games last just 40 minutes. There is a half-time break and

(13) .... side can take one 'time-out' per half. This is **(14)** .... the clock is stopped for one minute, similar to **(15)** .... happens in a basketball match. The game is particularly good for young people, **(16)** .... it encourages them to be creative and develop techniques in a small space, all of which is helpful in eleven-a-side football, which many futsal players go on to play.

For questions **17–24**, read the text below. Use the word given in capitals at the end of some of the lines to form a word that fits in the gap **in the same line**. There is an example at the beginning (**0**).

Write your answers **IN CAPITAL LETTERS on the separate answer sheet**.

Example: | **0** | E | X | A | C | T | L | Y | | | | | | | | | | | | |

Peanut butter is good for you!

With 'peanuts' and 'butter' in its name, peanut butter doesn't **(0)** ....   **EXACT**

sound good for us. Common sense tells us that neither food is a particularly

healthy **(17)** .... given their high fat content. The product's   **CHOOSE**

(18) .... , however, has led to research, and it's good news to learn   **POPULAR**

that many food science **(19)** .... say it isn't as bad for us as we might   **SPECIAL**

have thought.

Peanut butter is **(20)** .... versatile – it can be eaten with   **DOUBT**

everything from raw vegetable sticks to toast – but the fat it contains is also

monounsaturated (the 'right' kind of fat), which is believed to be good for the

heart. Peanut butter also contains a **(21)** .... amount of protein, which   **SUBSTANCE**

contains important nutrients for growing kids. **(22)** .... , it contains   **ADD**

iron, B vitamins and fibre, all of which are necessary for the **(23)** ....   **MAINTAIN**

of a healthy body. So, next time you're told to put the top back on the jar, you'll

be able to offer an **(24)** .... as to why just one more spoonful is good   **EXPLAIN**

for you!

For questions **25–30**, complete the second sentence so that it has a similar meaning to the first sentence, using the word given. **Do not change the word given**. You must use between **two** and **five** words, including the word given. Here is an example (**0**).

Example:

0   I haven't seen you for ages!

TIME

It has .... I saw you!

The gap can be filled by the words 'been a long time since', so you write:

Example: | **0** | BEEN A LONG TIME SINCE |

Write only the missing words **IN CAPITAL LETTERS on the separate answer sheet**.

---

25   I meant to call you when I arrived at the hotel but I forgot.
GOING
I .... you a call when I arrived at the hotel but I forgot.

26   'What do you think of the amount footballers get paid?' Tim asked me.
THOUGHT
Tim .... about the amount footballers get paid.

27   It'll be dark soon, so we mustn't stay out any longer.
LEAVE
We'd .... gets dark.

28   We hadn't expected the party to be very good but in the end it was!
TURNED
The party .... than we had expected.

29   We won't be going on holiday this year because we haven't got enough money.
LACK
Our .... that we won't be going on holiday this year.

30   The team won the match even though they hadn't practised much.
IN
The team won the match .... practised much.

You are going to read a magazine article written by a boy who went to a festival called La Mercè in Spain. For questions **31–36**, choose the answer (**A**, **B**, **C** or **D**) which you think fits best according to the text.

Mark your answers **on the separate answer sheet**.

La Mercè Festival

by Adrian Jacobs

Last September, I attended the La Mercè festival in the city of Barcelona, Spain, with my family. I'd never been to the city before and was looking forward to spending a few days there. After checking in to our hotel, we wandered into the centre for our first look around the city I'd heard so much about. With the festival already in full swing, the footpaths were crowded, making it challenging to move with any speed around the sights. It was nothing I hadn't been warned about and we were in no rush. I could barely take my eyes off the beautiful old buildings as we walked along. All that fascinating history: I imagined all the stories the buildings would be able to tell if they had a voice. Traffic buzzed round us, filling the air with sounds of beeping horns, adding to the atmosphere.

The first event we attended was the building of 'human towers'. Different teams competed to create the tallest tower of people by standing on each others' shoulders. Then the youngest member of each group climbed up the outside to the very top. I gazed in awe at the height of the towers. They made it look easy but what an incredible amount of practice and teamwork the activity must need. Now and then, a tower would collapse to the gasps of the onlookers. The teams had clearly prepared for this eventuality, though, and caught each other easily. We stood and watched for ages, transfixed.

Next was the parade of the 'giants', where huge brightly painted figures were carried through the streets representing different neighbourhoods of the city. Kings and queens dressed in historical costumes hovered over the crowds, spinning and dancing in pairs to the tunes played on ancient instruments by bands of musicians. Children stared in wonder, their faces lighting up when they spotted a favourite character – that was a magical thing. I soon abandoned any attempt at filming the procession; it was far better just to store the images away in my memory instead.

That evening we saw what, for me, was the highlight of our whole trip: the 'fire run'. Another parade, but this one was a procession of huge fire-breathing beasts – again, brightly painted – which were carried along the road, showering the spectators with sparks from fireworks attached to them. Spectators are advised to cover up as protection, but there's no real danger. Even so, I decided to stand well back away from it! It was an incredible sight and must have been great fun to participate in. The fire lit up the spectators in the darkness and I recognised my own feelings of happiness on their faces. I snapped away with my camera, but when I looked at my pictures the next day, I'd just recorded a blur of movement.

Over the next couple of days we saw everything from a kite flying competition at the beach to an aerobatic show, sampled local specialities in seaside cafés and sang and *line 52* danced in the city's numerous squares. All too soon it was the last night of the festival. Together with thousands of other people, we stood ready to watch the final event: the closing of the festival with a magnificent fireworks display. It was as fantastic as all the other events had been and I knew that even if I never came back again, I'd go home having made the most of the celebrations I'd so longed to see, and having gained an insight into another culture.

31 How did Adrian feel when he saw the city of Barcelona for the first time?

    A   amazed at the number of visitors there
    B   excited by the interesting architecture
    C   annoyed by how noisy the city was
    D   pleased about how easy it was to get around

32 What does Adrian say about the 'human towers' event in the second paragraph?

    A   It made him feel nervous at certain moments.
    B   It continued for longer than he would have liked.
    C   It required a lot of skill on the part of the participants.
    D   It was not as impressive as he had expected it to be.

33 When Adrian saw the parade of giants in the third paragraph, he particularly liked

    A   trying to capture the figures on video.
    B   seeing other people's enjoyment of it.
    C   learning about the history of the activity.
    D   listening to the music which accompanied it.

34 During the 'fire run' in the fourth paragraph, Adrian

    A   thought it wise to keep at a distance from the parade.
    B   wished he was able to take part in the procession.
    C   managed to take some atmospheric photos.
    D   saw someone he knew in the crowds.

35 What does *sampled* in line 52 mean?

    A   checked
    B   experimented
    C   observed
    D   tried

36 How did Adrian feel at the end of the festival?

    A   hopeful that he would return in the future
    B   regretful that the experience was over
    C   satisfied to have fulfilled an ambition
    D   happy to be heading home

You are going to read a newspaper article about a girl called Carly, who has taken part in a scheme called the Young Businessperson at school. Six sentences have been removed from the article. Choose from the sentences **A–G** the one which fits each gap (**37–42**). There is one extra sentence which you do not need to use.

Mark your answers **on the separate answer sheet**.

Taking part in the Young Businessperson scheme

14-year-old Carly Smithson reports on taking part in the Young Businessperson scheme at school

The aim of the Young Businessperson scheme was to give young people like my classmates and I a taste of what it's like running a business, providing an insight into the world of work, and raising awareness of the skills needed in the real world that can't be learnt in academic lessons, such as handling money and keeping records.

We were going to work in teams to set up and run small, and hopefully profitable, businesses from school. The first thing we did was attend a workshop with the scheme's leader, Matt. He encouraged us to think about businesses we might be able to create and manage with limited resources. **37** [ ] Take shoelaces. They stop your shoes slipping off, but also allow people to fasten their shoes comfortably, regardless of how big their feet are. It's a simple idea, but imagine how many pairs of laces there are, and how much money must be made from sales!

We spent the first half of the workshop coming up with problems we encounter in our daily lives. I find it annoying when food packets tear in the wrong place when you open them, so the food inside spills out or goes off more quickly than if it would if the packet could be re-sealed. **38** [ ] Matt then split us into smaller groups to choose one of the problems and consider a possible solution for it. My group worked on what I'd mentioned, and our suggestion was to create snack packets which could be re-fastened.

39 [ ] 'But think about how much more expensive it would be than producing current kinds of packet,' he said. 'More resources would be needed so

manufacturing costs would be higher. They'd take longer to make, too. Then there are existing products on the market, such as boxes with lids, which people can use and re-use for this purpose.' He wasn't being unkind, I realised, but pointing out considerations businesses have to make in order to make a profit.

It was a useful exercise aimed at developing our 'business heads'. Plus, we could never have made the packets at school without specialist machinery and equipment. **40** [ ] In the end, our group came up with a glove for washing dishes which would not only protect hands from hot water, but prevent the inconvenience of having to search around in the water to find a dropped cloth. Matt approved it, and our group was given a small amount of money with which to buy essential materials.

In addition to making the gloves, each person was assigned a specific role. **41** [ ] This would be used for promotional purposes, and to make sure every member of the group could explain things consistently to customers. We had a few minor disagreements along the way, but even those were no bad thing as we learnt to compromise and resolve conflict.

It was when we came to selling our products that we came up against our first real problem: not many of our classmates wanted a washing-up glove! We sold more to teachers than other students. **42** [ ] Matt was positive about that, though. He said we'd learnt a good lesson: we hadn't thought about the needs of our target market. He praised us on our teamwork, though, and said he'd recommend any of us for jobs in the future!'

A He was pleased we'd tried to be more ambitious than other groups.

B We should have chosen something more straightforward, and that's what we decided to do next.

C Although we covered our costs, we made very little profit, which was disappointing.

D Successful organisations often offer a solution to a problem, we learnt.

E When we fed back our ideas, Matt wasn't as enthusiastic as we'd hoped.

F Other students shared their experiences and mentioned other minor but frustrating issues.

G I was responsible for creating an accurate description of our product.

You are going to read four reviews by teenagers of documentaries they have watched. For questions **43–52**, choose from the reviewers (**A–D**). The reviewers may be chosen more than once.

Mark your answers **on the separate answer sheet**.

Which reviewer

managed to gain some of the knowledge they had hoped/expected to?	43
was pleased with the outcome of someone's efforts shown in the programme?	44
says they were inspired to take action after watching the programme?	45
believes that certain facts about a subject will never be revealed?	46
realised something they had been doing wrong before seeing the programme?	47
says they admired the way a programme presented its special effects?	48
was initially unwilling to watch the programme?	49
was disappointed with one aspect of the programme they saw?	50
corrects something they have said earlier in their review?	51
says they regret not having taken more notice of a subject when they had the chance?	52

TV documentaries

A   Dan Parker reviews *Polar bear*

I saw *Polar bear* with my whole family and I was impressed by how it managed to get across some quite complicated information in a way that even my sister, who's a few years younger than me, could understand. I didn't feel talked down to, either, like I sometimes do: some documentaries provide only the most basic facts about an issue and you're often left with lots of unanswered questions. *Polar bear* approached the subject of global warming in a fascinating way. A polar bear was tracked for a year and we saw its habitat through its own eyes, observing how it tried to adapt to new challenges and seeing first-hand the impact on its life that melting ice is having. I felt more determined than ever to get involved in raising awareness about these issues, and I signed up to a local environmental group for young people straightaway.

B   Nelly Jones reviews *Practice makes perfect*

I love playing basketball but I never seem to get any better, no matter how hard I'm working. Maybe that should be no matter how hard I *think* I'm working. That was the point of *Practice makes perfect*. It documented a percussionist called Rob, who wanted to get a place in an orchestra but just wasn't making it, even though he'd been to a ton of auditions and was an amazing player. An expert observed him practising one day and noticed that Rob was playing rhythms he was so familiar with that he wasn't really thinking about them. He was advised to do something called 'purposeful practice' – concentrating on what he was doing and trying to do it better. It was a real eye-opener for me and I understood why I hadn't improved my game for ages. Oh, and after spending time with the expert, Rob got his dream job! That was the coolest bit.

C   Lucas Martin reviews *Dinosaurs*

I've never really been into dinosaurs and I wasn't in the least interested in watching another documentary about them. My family wanted to see it so I just thought, 'Well, I've got nothing to lose'. I was instantly hooked! The special effects were incredible as they often are in those kinds of programme, but I started thinking about how much the film-makers actually knew, and how much was simply guesswork on their part. How did they know what colour dinosaurs were? Is that really how the creatures moved? These are all things that to my knowledge are too late to discover. I thought I'd learnt everything there was to know about the different kinds of dinosaur but when the presenter mentioned that there'd been hundreds of kinds I was pretty shocked. How come I hadn't known that? Perhaps I hadn't paid enough attention at school. I definitely should have.

D   Hayley Vickers reviews *Making changes*

The minute I saw this programme advertised, I knew I had to watch it. I'm really into making films about issues which affect young people, and I'm always looking for ways to improve my skills or present stuff in an attention-grabbing kind of way. The subject matter of *Making changes* was already appealing (it was about the power of advertising and how it can be used for the greater good), but it also focused on new media and I thought I could pick up a few tips about getting messages across so that young people like me can get their ideas heard in an adult world. The programme was interesting, but although I did learn one or two things about improving my filming, I felt the content was a bit repetitive. It was still worth watching, though.

You **must** answer this question. Write your answer in **140–190** words in an appropriate style **on the separate answer sheet**.

1   In your English class you have been talking about fashion. Now your English teacher has asked you to write an essay.

Write your essay using **all** the notes and giving reasons for your point of view.

Some teenagers make a big effort to be fashionable. Is this a good thing?

Notes

Write about:

1. feeling confident

2. effect of advertisements

3. .... (your own idea)

Write an answer to **one** of the questions **2–5** in this part. Write your answer in **140–190** words in an appropriate style **on the separate answer sheet**. Put the question number in the box at the top of the answer sheet.

2   You have received this email from your English-speaking friend, Ella.

Reply   Forward

> My family always have holidays in the UK, but I want to travel abroad instead! Do you agree that it is a good idea to travel and see other countries? How can I persuade my parents to go somewhere different this summer?

Write your **email**.

3   You have seen see this announcement in an English-language magazine for teenagers.

> ***Articles wanted!***
>
> **An amazing person**
>
> Tell us about someone amazing. It could be someone famous, or someone you know. Why do you think this person is so wonderful? What have you learnt from this person?
>
> The best articles will appear on our website!

Write your **article**.

4   You see this announcement on an English-language website for young people.

> ***Reviews wanted!***
>
> **Favourite games**
>
> We want to know about a game you play. It could be a computer game, a board game or another kind of game. Describe the game briefly. Who do you play it with? Why do you enjoy playing it? Would you recommend it to other people your age?
>
> The best reviews will win a game!

Write your **review**.

5   Answer the following question based on the set text.

You have been talking about the set text in your English class. Now your teacher has given you this essay for homework:

What did you think was the most surprising event in the book? Why was it so surprising? What were the results of this event?

Write your **essay**.

🎧43) You will hear people talking in eight different situations. For questions **1–8**, choose the best answer (**A, B** or **C**).

1   You hear two friends talking about some changes at their school.
    What do they agree?

    A   Certain rules haven't changed in the way they'd hoped.
    B   The changes will make part of their daily routine easier.
    C   More interesting activities will be on offer as a result.

2   You hear a girl talking to a friend about the library in their town.
    During the conversation, she

    A   criticises the range of books in the library.
    B   suggests how the library could be improved.
    C   describes a library book she's read recently.

3   You hear two friends discussing a concert they've just been to.
    What do they agree about it?

    A   The band didn't play enough well-known songs.
    B   One player's performance wasn't what they'd expected.
    C   The venue wasn't ideal for the event.

4   You hear a teacher telling her class about a design task they are going to work on.
    What is she doing?

    A   advising them which kind of designs will work best
    B   reminding them of the possible risks of using the machines
    C   suggesting key steps for achieving their goal

5   You hear a girl leaving a voicemail message for her friend.
    Why is she calling her?

    A   to apologise for not ringing her as arranged
    B   to propose ways of helping her while she's off sick
    C   to try and find out the details of her injury

6   You hear a boy talking to a friend about a meal he cooked for his family last night.
    What does he admit about the meal?

    A   He hadn't realised how little food the recipe would make.
    B   He should have checked that his family would like the meal.
    C   He was too ambitious in his choice of recipe.

7   You hear a girl talking about her first piano lesson.
    How did she feel about it?

    A   confident that she'd pick it up quickly
    B   concerned at the extent of the task ahead
    C   surprised at how unfamiliar the instrument was

8   You hear two friends talking about a new music shop in their town.
    What do they think is unusual about the shop?

    A   It offers huge reductions on some items.
    B   It stocks music from their parents' era.
    C   It has regular visits from famous musicians.

🎧 44 You will hear a boy called Jack giving a talk about his visit to a castle in the summer holidays. For questions **9–18**, complete the sentences with a word or short phrase.

A castle visit

Jack's route to the castle involved a path near the edge of a **(9)** ....

Jack uses the word **(10)** .... to describe his first impression of the castle.

Jack discovered that the remains of an earlier castle made of **(11)** .... could still be seen.

Jack was surprised by the **(12)** .... of the castle walls as they walked along the top of them.

Jack was amazed at the view from the part of the castle called the **(13)** .... that he visited.

Jack learnt that many improvements to the castle had been made by the **(14)** .... of a previous owner.

Jack's father most enjoyed seeing the restored **(15)** .... inside the castle.

Jack decided he didn't believe the guide's story about **(16)** .... in one area of the castle.

Jack and his family were impressed by the **(17)** .... display that they saw.

Jack felt the **(18)** .... in one of the gardens created a peaceful atmosphere.

🎧45 You will hear five teenagers talking about their favourite wildlife programmes. For questions **19–23**, choose from the list (**A–H**) what each speaker particularly likes about the programme. Use the letters only once. There are three extra letters which you do not need to use.

A   It's made me aware of threats to our environment.

B   It's presented by wildlife experts.

Speaker 1 | 19 |

C   It has beautiful photography.

Speaker 2 | 20 |

D   It's taught me about some unusual species.

Speaker 3 | 21 |

E   It's inspired me to get involved with nature.

Speaker 4 | 22 |

F   It helps me with my schoolwork.

G   It promotes research into conservation.

Speaker 5 | 23 |

H   It features wildlife from my area.

🎧 46 You will hear an interview with a student called Katie Cross, who is talking about her hobby of kitesurfing. For questions **24–30**, choose the best answer (**A, B** or **C**).

24 Katie says that for her, kitesurfing

    A   is something she wishes she could do more of.

    B   is great motivation for completing her school work.

    C   is a better alternative for keeping fit than running.

25 What advantage of the sport does Katie point out?

    A   It's relatively low-cost at the beginning.

    B   It's easy to find somewhere to do it.

    C   It's possible to transport the kit yourself.

26 What surprised Katie about the sport the first time she tried it?

    A   It didn't require as much strength as she'd expected.

    B   It wasn't only a sport for young people.

    C   It didn't seem as tiring as people had told her.

27 What does Katie suggest about her rapid progress in kitesurfing?

    A   She thinks she was naturally talented at it.

    B   Her rate of improvement wasn't unusual.

    C   She succeeded due to her determination.

28 What does Katie particularly appreciate about kitesurfers she's met?

    A   They encourage her to improve by being so competitive.

    B   They're all very friendly towards each other.

    C   They tend to have a lot of experience in watersports.

29 Katie recommends that people who want to try kitesurfing should

    A   learn how to deal with different sea conditions.

    B   learn to control the kite they're using properly.

    C   learn from a professional instructor.

30 Katie is currently preparing to

    A   take part in some competitions.

    B   go abroad on a kitesurfing holiday.

    C   train to teach others how to kitesurf.

Part 1   2 minutes [3 minutes for groups of three]

Interlocutor   First we'd like to know something about you.

Travelling around

- Do you prefer to travel by bus or by car? (Why?)
- What do you like to do on a long journey? (Why?)
- Tell us about the most interesting journey you've ever taken.
- What's the best way to travel around the place where you live? (Why?)
- Do you often go cycling? (Why? / Why not?)

Part 2   4 minutes [6 minutes for groups of three]

Interlocutor   In this part of the test, I'm going to give each of you two photographs. I'd like you to talk about your photographs on your own for about a minute, and also to answer a question about your partner's photographs.

(*Candidate A*), it's your turn first. Here are your photographs on page C21 of the Speaking appendix. They show **people learning to do different things**.

I'd like you to compare the photographs, and say **why you think the people are learning to do these things**.

All right?

Candidate A
🕐 *1 minute* ....

Interlocutor   Thank you.

(*Candidate B*), **which of these things would you prefer to learn? (Why?)**

Candidate B
🕐 *Approximately 30 seconds* ....

Interlocutor   Thank you.

Now, (*Candidate B*), here are your photographs on page C22 of the Speaking appendix. They show **people doing different outdoor activities**.

I'd like you to compare the photographs, and say **what you think the people are enjoying about doing these outdoor activities**. All right?

Candidate B
🕐 *1 minute* ....

Interlocutor   Thank you.

(*Candidate A*), **which of these activities would you prefer to do? (Why?)**

Candidate A
🕐 *Approximately 30 seconds* ....

Interlocutor   Thank you.

Interlocutor Now I'd like you to talk about something together for about two minutes.

Some people think it's better to do everything with friends, and other people disagree. Here are some ideas of activities and a question for you to discuss.

First you have some time to look at the task on page C23 of the Speaking appendix.

Now talk to each other about **whether it's better to do these activities with friends or alone**.

Candidates

🕐 *2 minutes (3 minutes for groups of three)*

Interlocutor Thank you. Now you have about a minute to decide **which is the most difficult thing to do alone**.

Candidates

🕐 *1 minute (for pairs and groups of three)*

Interlocutor Thank you.

Part 4   4 minutes [6 minutes for groups of three]

Interlocutor

- Do you think it's easier to do something difficult if you're part of a team? (Why? / Why not?)

- Is it a good idea for schools to take students on school trips? (Why? / Why not?)

- If you want to be good friends with someone, is it necessary to share their interests? (Why? / Why not?)

- Some people say it's always better to make your own decisions about everything. Do you agree? (Why? / Why not?)

- Do you think it's better to get advice from friends or family? (Why?)

- Some people think it's important to spend some time on your own every day. What do you think? (Why?

Thank you. That is the end of the test.

> **What do you think?**
> **Do you agree?**
> **And you?**

Reading and Use of English

17927

CAMBRIDGE ENGLISH
Language Assessment
Part of the University of Cambridge

Candidate Name		Candidate Number	
Centre Name		Centre Number	
Examination Title		Examination Details	
Candidate Signature		Assessment Date	

Supervisor: If the candidate is ABSENT or has WITHDRAWN shade here ○

FCE for Schools Reading and Use of English Candidate Answer Sheet

Instructions

Use a PENCIL (B or HB).
Rub out any answer you want to change using an eraser.

Parts 1, 5, 6 and 7:
Mark ONE letter for each question.

For example, if you think A is the right answer to the question, mark your answer sheet like this:

Parts 2, 3 and 4: Write your answer clearly in CAPITAL LETTERS.

For parts 2 and 3, write one letter in each box.   0 EXAMPLE 1

Part 1

	A	B	C	D
1	○	○	○	○
2	○	○	○	○
3	○	○	○	○
4	○	○	○	○
5	○	○	○	○
6	○	○	○	○
7	○	○	○	○
8	○	○	○	○

Part 2

Do not write below here

9		9 1 0 ○ ○
10		10 1 0 ○ ○
11		11 1 0 ○ ○
12		12 1 0 ○ ○
13		13 1 0 ○ ○
14		14 1 0 ○ ○
15		15 1 0 ○ ○
16		16 1 0 ○ ○

Continues over ➡

17927

Reading and Use of English

17927

Part 3

	Do not write below here
17	17 **1** **0** ○ ○
18	18 **1** **0** ○ ○
19	19 **1** **0** ○ ○
20	20 **1** **0** ○ ○
21	21 **1** **0** ○ ○
22	22 **1** **0** ○ ○
23	23 **1** **0** ○ ○
24	24 **1** **0** ○ ○

Part 4

	Do not write below here
25	25 **2** **1** **0** ○ ○ ○
26	26 **2** **1** **0** ○ ○ ○
27	27 **2** **1** **0** ○ ○ ○
28	28 **2** **1** **0** ○ ○ ○
29	29 **2** **1** **0** ○ ○ ○
30	30 **2** **1** **0** ○ ○ ○

Part 5

	A	B	C	D
31	○	○	○	○
32	○	○	○	○
33	○	○	○	○
34	○	○	○	○
35	○	○	○	○
36	○	○	○	○

Part 6

	A	B	C	D	E	F	G
37	○	○	○	○	○	○	○
38	○	○	○	○	○	○	○
39	○	○	○	○	○	○	○
40	○	○	○	○	○	○	○
41	○	○	○	○	○	○	○
42	○	○	○	○	○	○	○

Part 7

	A	B	C	D	E	F
43	○	○	○	○	○	○
44	○	○	○	○	○	○
45	○	○	○	○	○	○
46	○	○	○	○	○	○
47	○	○	○	○	○	○
48	○	○	○	○	○	○
49	○	○	○	○	○	○
50	○	○	○	○	○	○
51	○	○	○	○	○	○
52	○	○	○	○	○	○

17927

   Photocopiable   **Sample answer sheets** | 183

Listening

18745

Part 1

	A	B	C			A	B	C
1	○	○	○		5	○	○	○
2	○	○	○		6	○	○	○
3	○	○	○		7	○	○	○
4	○	○	○		8	○	○	○

Part 2 (Remember to write in CAPITAL LETTERS or numbers)

		Do not write below here
9		9 1 0 ○ ○
10		10 1 0 ○ ○
11		11 1 0 ○ ○
12		12 1 0 ○ ○
13		13 1 0 ○ ○
14		14 1 0 ○ ○
15		15 1 0 ○ ○
16		16 1 0 ○ ○
17		17 1 0 ○ ○
18		18 1 0 ○ ○

Part 3

	A	B	C	D	E	F	G	H
19	○	○	○	○	○	○	○	○
20	○	○	○	○	○	○	○	○
21	○	○	○	○	○	○	○	○
22	○	○	○	○	○	○	○	○
23	○	○	○	○	○	○	○	○

Part 4

	A	B	C
24	○	○	○
25	○	○	○
26	○	○	○
27	○	○	○
28	○	○	○
29	○	○	○
30	○	○	○

18745

Speaking

29607

CAMBRIDGE ENGLISH
Language Assessment
Part of the University of Cambridge

Candidate Name		Candidate Number	
Centre Name		Centre Number	
Examination Title		Examination Details	
		Assessment Date	

Supervisor: If the candidate is ABSENT or has WITHDRAWN shade here ○

FCE for Schools Speaking Mark Sheet

Date of test:

Month: 1 2 3 4 5 6 7 8 9 10 11 12
○ ○ ○ ○ ○ ○ ○ ○ ○ ○ ○ ○

Day: 1 2 3 4 5 6 7 8 9 10 11 12 13 14 15 16 17 18 19 20 21 22 23 24 25 26 27 28 29 30 31
○ ○

Marks Awarded:

	0	1.0	1.5	2.0	2.5	3.0	3.5	4.0	4.5	5.0
Grammar and Vocabulary	○	○	○	○	○	○	○	○	○	○
Discourse Management	○	○	○	○	○	○	○	○	○	○
Pronunciation	○	○	○	○	○	○	○	○	○	○
Interactive Communication	○	○	○	○	○	○	○	○	○	○
Global Achievement	○	○	○	○	○	○	○	○	○	○

Test materials used:

Part 2 1 2 3 4 5 6 7 8 9 10 11 12 13 14 15 16 17 18 19 20
○ ○ ○ ○ ○ ○ ○ ○ ○ ○ ○ ○ ○ ○ ○ ○ ○ ○ ○ ○

Part 3 21 22 23 24 25 26 27 28 29 30
○ ○ ○ ○ ○ ○ ○ ○ ○ ○

Assessor's number

Test Format
Examiners:Candidates

2 : 2
○

Number of 2nd Candidate

Interlocutor's number

2 : 3
○

Number of 3rd Candidate

29607

Acknowledgements

Our highly experienced team of Trainer writers, in collaboration with Cambridge English Language Assessment reviewers, have worked together to bring you *First for Schools Trainer 2*. We would like to thank Helen Chilton (writer), Nick Cherkas (writer), Anthony Cosgrove (writer), Jeremy Day (writer), Sue Elliott (writer), Stephen Green (writer), Jacky Newbrook (writer), Helen Tiliouine (writer and reviewer) and Sarah Dymond (reviewer) for their work on the material.

The authors and publishers acknowledge the following sources of copyright material and are grateful for the permissions granted. While every effort has been made, it has not always been possible to identify the sources of all the material used, or to trace all copyright holders. If any omissions are brought to our notice, we will be happy to include the appropriate acknowledgements on reprinting and in the next update to the digital edition, as applicable.

Text Acknowledgements:
Telegraph Group Media Limited for the text on p. 151 adapted from 'High achiever: George Atkinson, record-breaking teenage mountaineer' by Chris Harvey, *The* Telegraph, 24.06.2011. Copyright © 2011 Telegraph Group Media Limited. Reproduced with permission.

Photo Acknowledgements:
All the photographs are sourced from Getty Images:
p. 10: aldomurillo/iStock/Getty Images Plus; p. 12: Viktorcvetkovic/E+; p. 13: Ayakovlev/iStock/Getty Images Plus; p. 14: Mike Harrington/Taxi; p. 15: Chris Ryan/OJO Images; p. 17: FatCamera/E+; p. 18: 33karen33/E+; p. 20: Thinkstock Images/Stockbyte; p. 21: Tim Macpherson/Cultura; p. 22: Clarissa Leahy/Cultura; p. 25: technotr/E+; P. 27: gbh00/iStock/Getty Images Plus; p. 29: wetcake/iStock/Getty Images Plus; p. 30: gjohnstonphoto/iStock/Getty Images Plus; p. 32: Eva-Katalin/E+; p. 33: Hill Street Studios/Blend Images; p. 44: GlobalP/iStock/Getty Images Plus; p. 65: belchonock/iStock/Getty Images Plus; p. 67: YakobchukOlena/iStock/Getty Images Plus; p. 68: Claire Cordier/Dorling Kindersley; p. 69: KidStock/Blend Images; p. 70: Corbis News; p. 72: LWA/Dann Tardif/Blend Images/Getty Images Plus; p. 73: leonardo255/iStock/Getty Images Plus; p. 74: Ariel Skelley/DigitalVision; p. 77: Highwaystarz-Photography/iStock/Getty Images Plus; p. 79: pixel107//iStock/Getty Images Plus; p. 80: Eva-Katalin/E+; p. 82: Btownchris/DigitalVision Vectors; p. 86: sturti/E+; p. 110: Westend61; p. 115: Photoplotnikov/GlobalP/iStock/Getty Images Plus; p. 128: Lucidio Studio Inc/Photographer's Choice RF; p. 129: duckycards/E+; p. 131: Rainer Dittrich; p. 146: Robert Morrissey/EyeEm; p. 147: wsfurlan/iStock/Getty Images Plus; p. 149: Hype Photography/Stone; p. 151: isoft/E+; p. 163: georgeclerk/iStock/Getty Images Plus; p. 164: Tuayai/iStock Editorial/Getty Images Plus; p. 165: matka_Wariatka/iStock/Getty Images Plus; p. 167: Sergi Escribano/Moment; C1 A: antolikjan/iStock/Getty Images Plus; C1 B: IR_Stone/iStock Editorial/Getty Images Plus; C2 A: dolgachov/iStock/Getty Images Plus; C2 B: Eva-Katalin/E+; C3 A: omgimages/iStock/Getty Images Plus; C3 B: M_a_y_a/E+; C4 A, B: monkeybusinessimages/iStock/Getty Images Plus; C8 A: Hero Images, C8 B: Amos Chapple/Lonely Planet Images; C9 A: oneinchpunch/iStock/Getty Images Plus; C9 B: Stewart Cohen/Blend Images; C10 A: martin-dm/E+; C10 B: SerrNovik/iStock/Getty Images Plus; C12 A: Marc Romanelli/Blend Images; C12 B: Zero Creatives/Cultura; C13 A: PamelaJoeMcFarlane/E+; C13 B: PamelaJoeMcFarlane/E+; C15 A: DragonImages/iStock/Getty Images Plus; C 15 B: Neustockimages/E+; C 16 A: Eva-Katalin/E+; C17 B: izusek/E+; C18 A: Tony Garcia/Image Source; C18 B: aldomurillo/iStock/Getty Images Plus; C19 A, B: monkeybusinessimages/iStock/Getty Images Plus; C21 A: dolgachov/iStock/Getty Images Plus; C21 B: kali9/E+; C 22 A: nullplus/iStock/Getty Images Plus; C22 B: Dave and Les Jacobs/Lloyd Dobbie/Blend Images.

Commissioned photography by Gareth Boden on p. 6, p. 60.
Commissioned photography by Trevor Clifford on p. 56, p. 57, p. 63.

Illustrations by:
Andrew Painter pp.4, 7–9.

Audio recordings by DN and AE Strauss Ltd. Engineer: Neil Rogers; Editor: James Miller; Producer: Dan Strauss. Recorded at Half Ton Studios, Cambridge

Why are the people outside at night?

A

B

What are the people enjoying about their tasks?

A

B

What are the friends enjoying about their day out?

A

B

Why have the people chosen to do exercise in these ways?

A

B

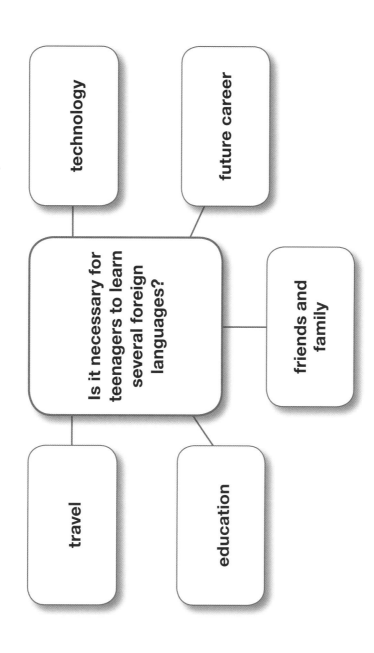

technology

future career

Is it necessary for teenagers to learn several foreign languages?

friends and family

travel

education

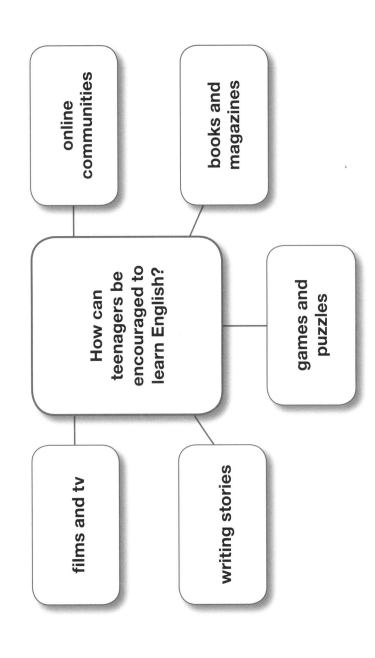

online communities

books and magazines

How can teenagers be encouraged to learn English?

games and puzzles

films and tv

writing stories

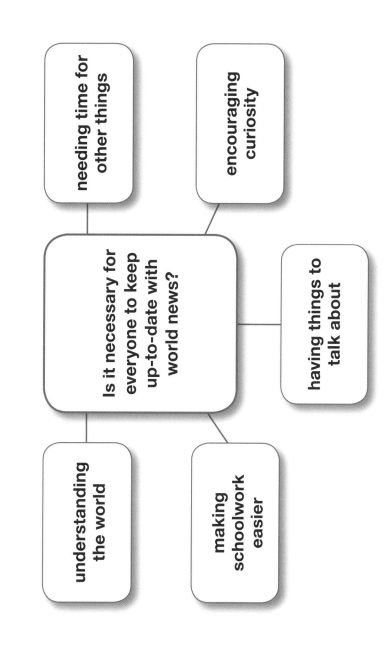

needing time for
other things

encouraging
curiosity

Is it necessary for
everyone to keep
up-to-date with
world news?

having things to
talk about

understanding
the world

making
schoolwork
easier

How are the people feeling about the snow?

A

B

Why are the people using mobile phones in these situations?

A

B

Why have the people chosen to read in these places?

A

B

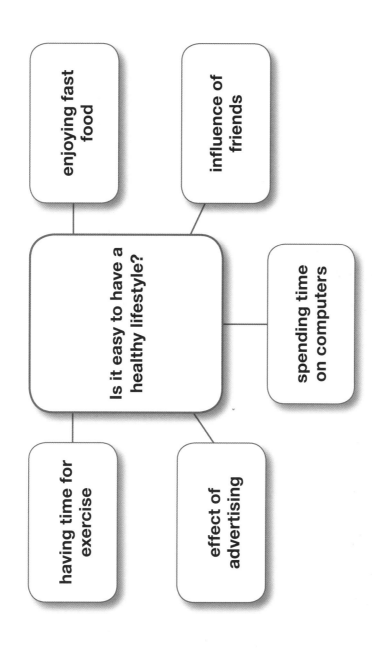

enjoying fast food

influence of friends

Is it easy to have a healthy lifestyle?

spending time on computers

having time for exercise

effect of advertising

What are the people enjoying about relaxing in these situations?

A

B

What are the people taking photographs in these situations?

A

B

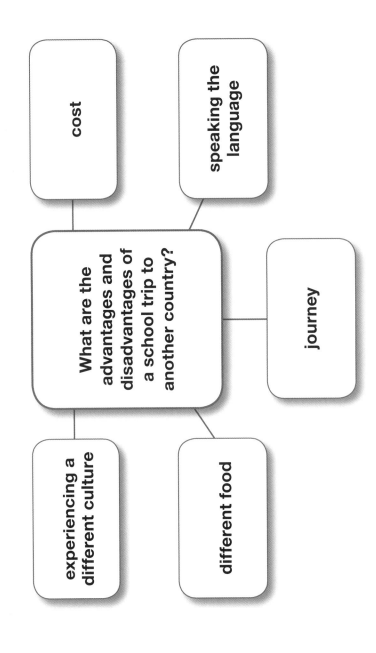

cost

speaking the language

What are the advantages and disadvantages of a school trip to another country?

journey

experiencing a different culture

different food

Why have the people decided to study in these places?

A

B

Why have the people chosen to travel in these ways?

A

B

Speaking Part 3

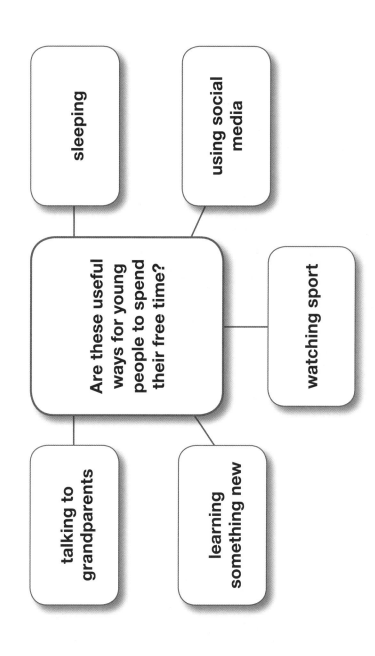

sleeping

using social media

Are these useful ways for young people to spend their free time?

watching sport

talking to grandparents

learning something new

What are the people enjoying about playing these games?

A

B

Why do the people need to concentrate in these situations?

A

B

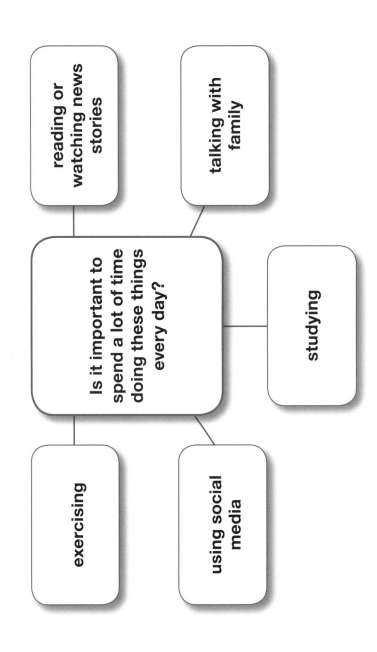

reading or watching news stories

talking with family

Is it important to spend a lot of time doing these things every day?

studying

exercising

using social media

Why are the people learning to do these things?

A

B

What are the people enjoying about doing these outdoor activities?

A

B

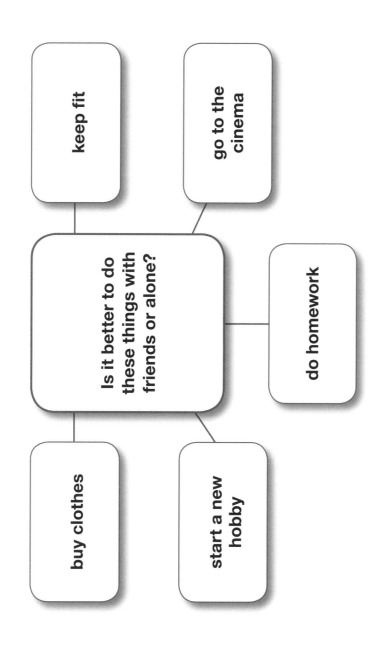

keep fit

go to the cinema

Is it better to do these things with friends or alone?

do homework

buy clothes

start a new hobby

Cambridge English

OFFICIAL EXAM PREPARATION MATERIALS

CAMBRIDGE.ORG/EXAMS

What do we do?

Together, Cambridge University Press and Cambridge English Language Assessment bring you official preparation materials for Cambridge English exams and IELTS.

What does *official* mean?

Our authors are experts in the exams they write for. In addition, all of our exam preparation is officially validated by the teams who produce the real exams.

Why else are our materials special?

Vocabulary is always 'on-level' as defined by the English Profile resource. Our materials are based on research from the Cambridge Learner Corpus to help students avoid common mistakes that exam candidates make.